The Healing Power of
WATER

The Healing Power of WATER

PHOTOGRAPHS BY MICHAEL KAHN

TEXT BY MICHAEL KAHN AND CHRISTINE YURICK

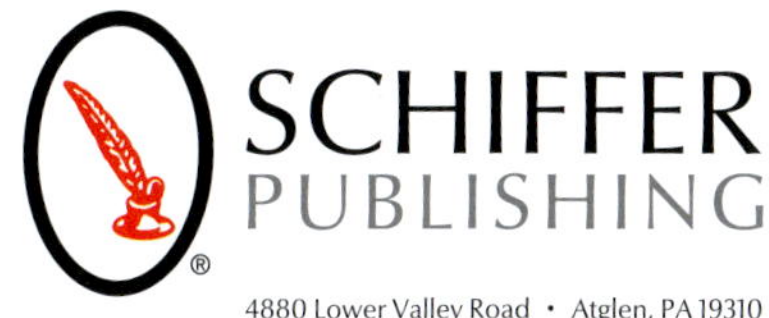

SCHIFFER PUBLISHING

4880 Lower Valley Road • Atglen, PA 19310

*To my editor and wife,
Christine Yurick, without whom
this book, and a lot of other things,
would never have happened.*

INTRODUCTION

All my life I have been drawn to water: streams, lakes, oceans, and ponds. Water is an endless source of inspiration because it is always changing. Heraclitus had it right when he said, "No man ever steps in the same river twice, for it's not the same river and he's not the same man."

Water can be a great teacher, too. Sitting along a stream, listening to the water flowing over the stones, moving through the riffles, or being on a beach with waves breaking on the shore creates a space between my thoughts where the truth is revealed, questions are answered, and an inner calm can come to the surface.

I am an avid sailor, and as any sailor knows, learning to accept what you cannot change is an important tool in navigating the waterways. The same is true in navigating our complex lives. Taking lessons from water teaches us about our own moods and mental states—we learn that when we feel agitated, we can look deeper and see the calm below. When the wind stops blowing, the water is still and, depending on the light, reflects the world around it or reveals glimpses of what lies beneath.

Using water to ground you can be helpful in bringing what is truly important to the surface. I have been lucky to combine my passion for water with my love of photography. Photography can happen only in the present moment. Nurturing your awareness and creating calm allows you to see your thoughts and desires for the future or regrets of the past as just that—thoughts. Being present in the now is where art happens. It is where healing happens. It is where magic happens.

I hope these images bring you joy and help you nurture your nature. Please remember that protecting water, and all of Earth's resources, is paramount to our survival.

Those who contemplate the beauty of the earth find reserves of strength that will endure as long as life lasts. There is something infinitely healing in the repeated refrains of nature—the assurance that dawn comes after night, and spring after winter.

—RACHEL CARSON

Let silence be the art you practice.

—RUMI

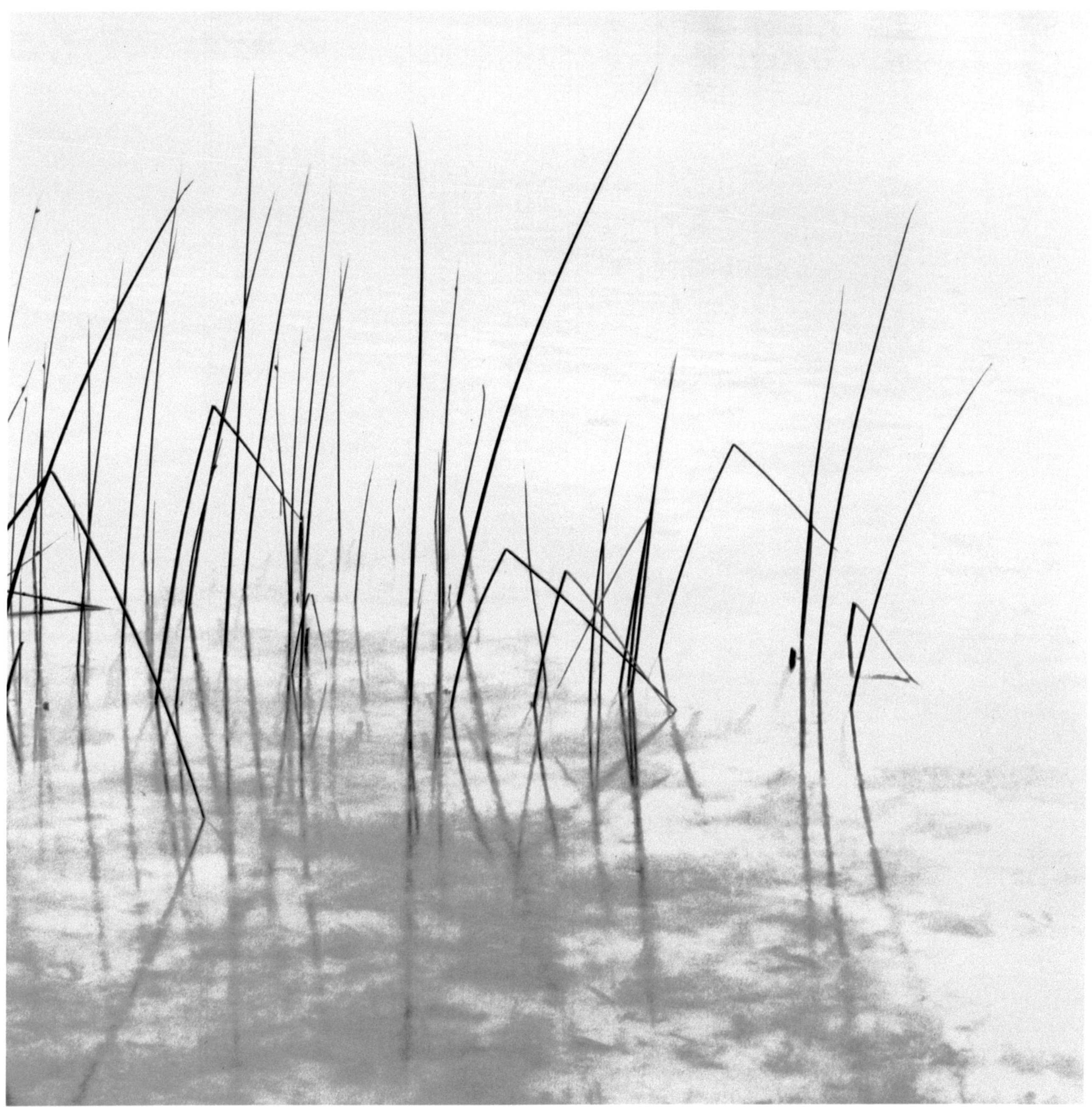

Otter Lake, Sleeping Bear Dunes National Park, Michigan, 2019

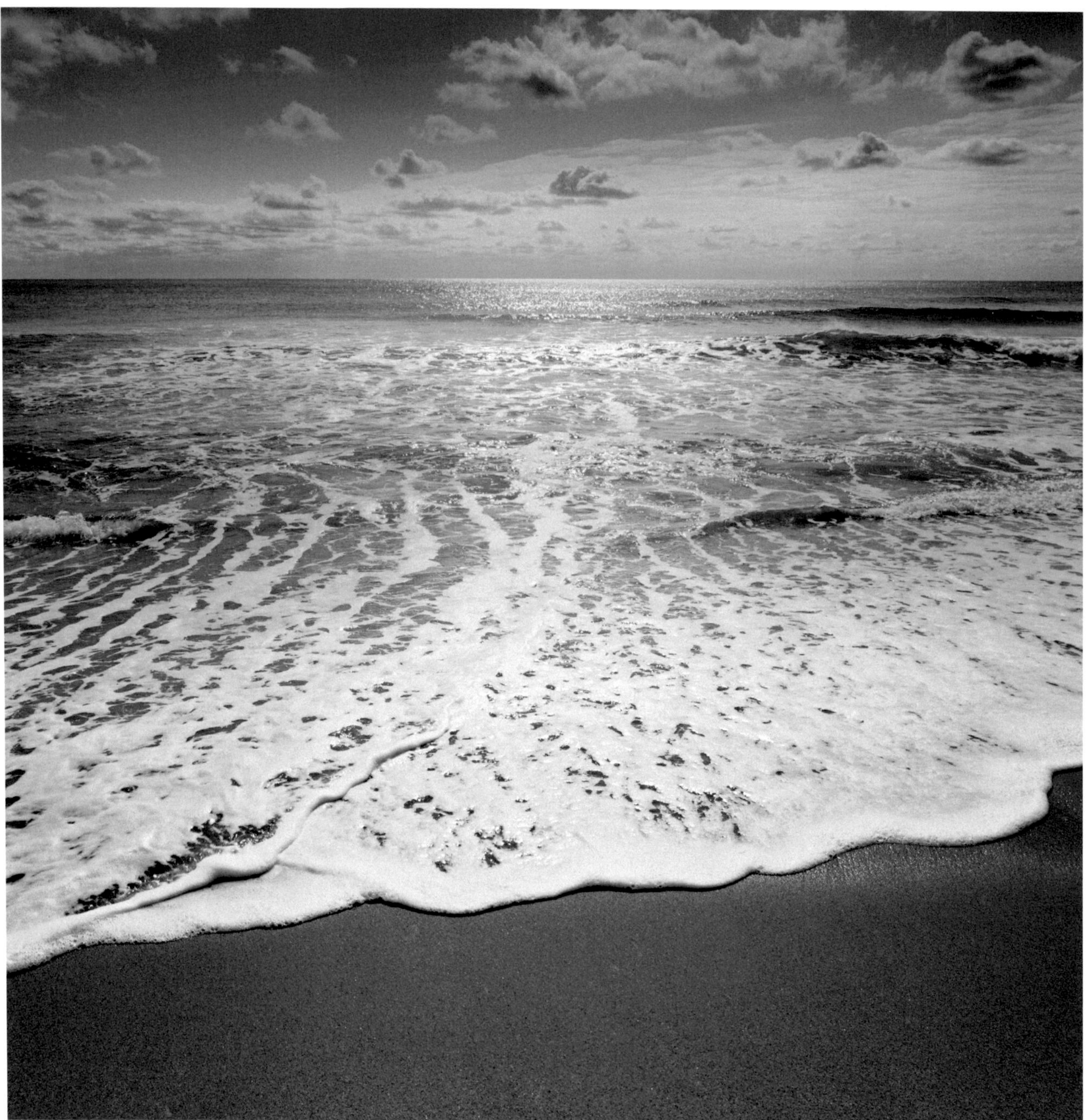

Martha's Vineyard, Massachusetts, 2006

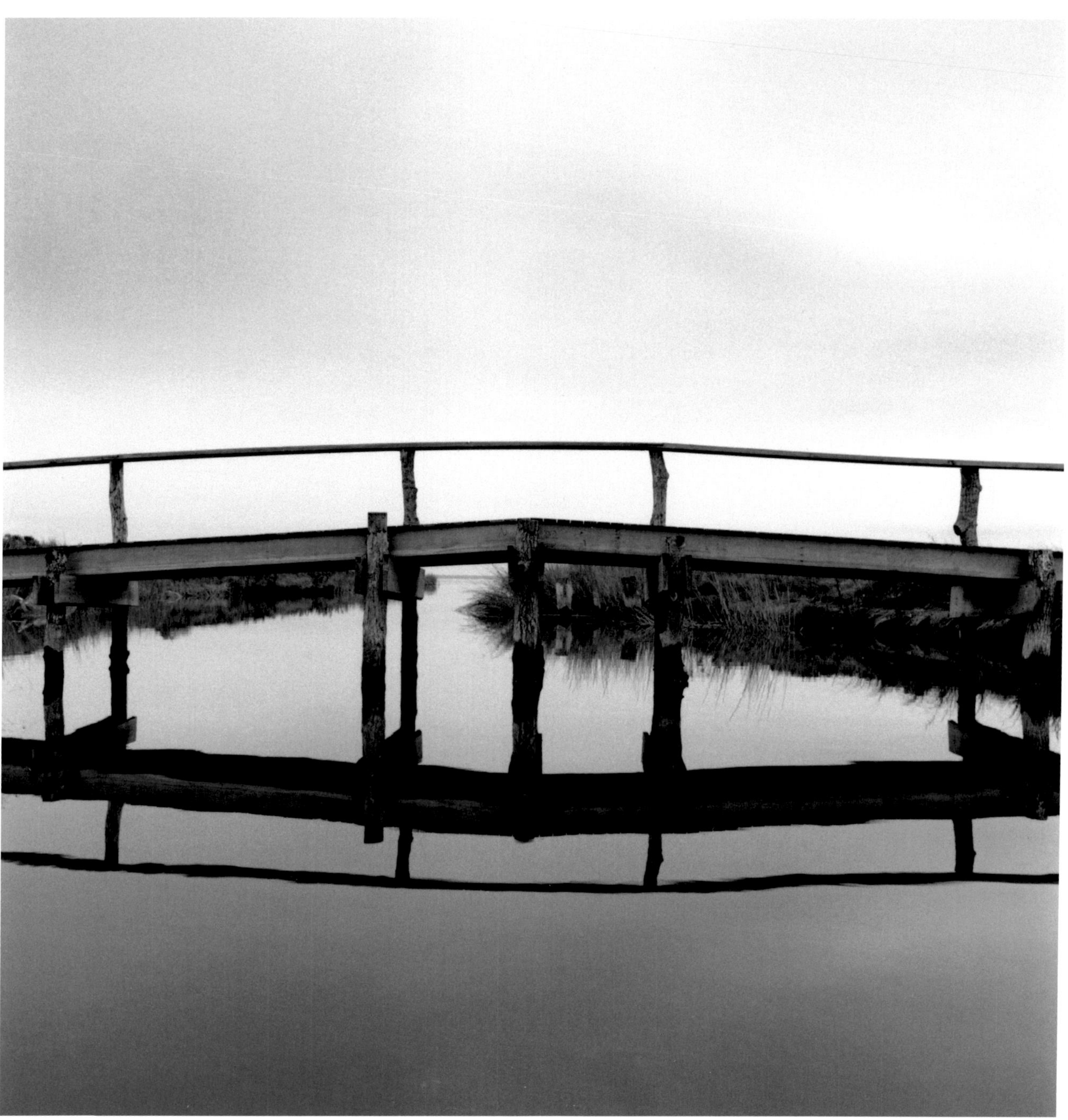

Martha's Vineyard, Massachusetts, 1999

People are capable, at any time in their lives, of doing what they dream of.

—PAULO COELHO

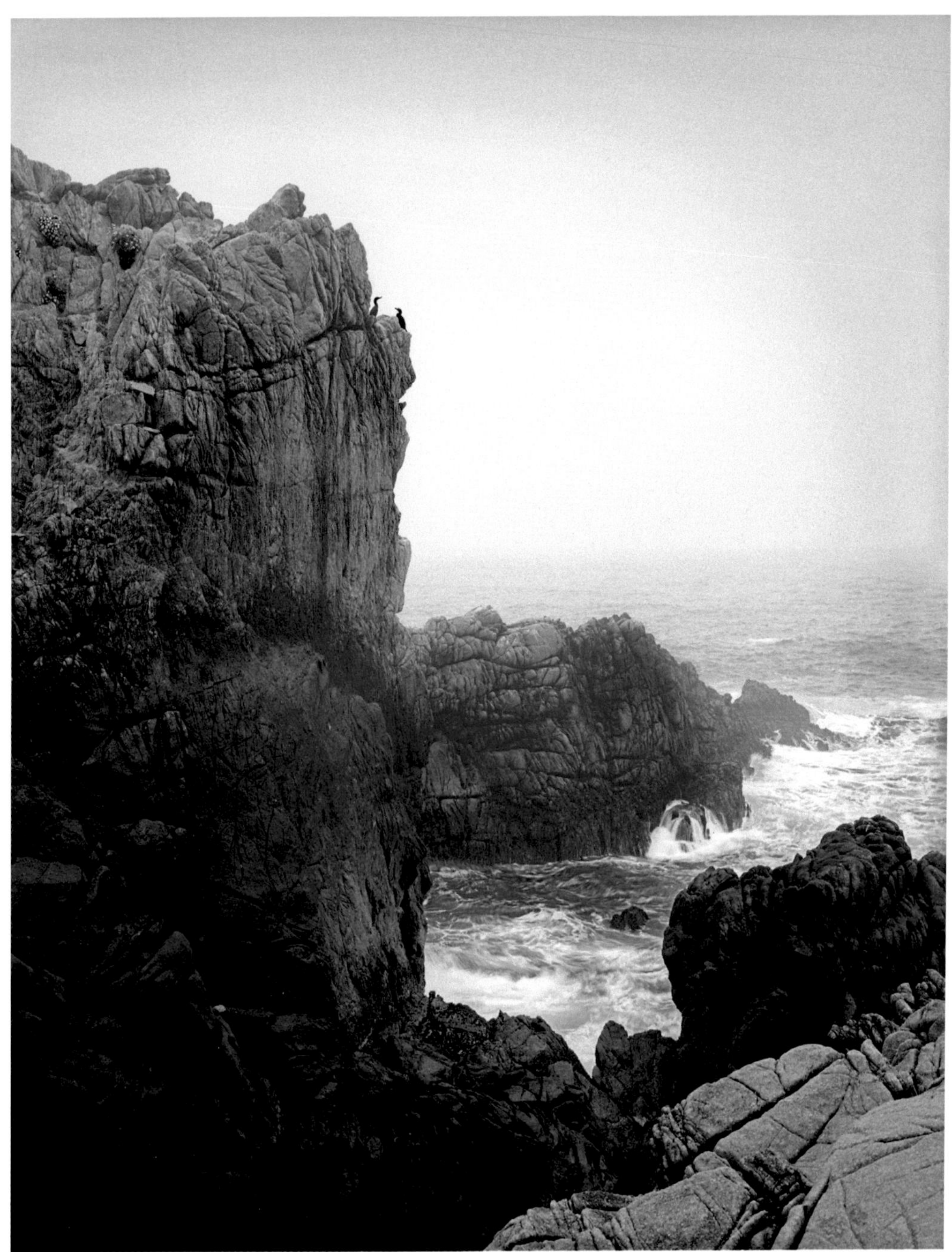

Point Lobos, California, 1999

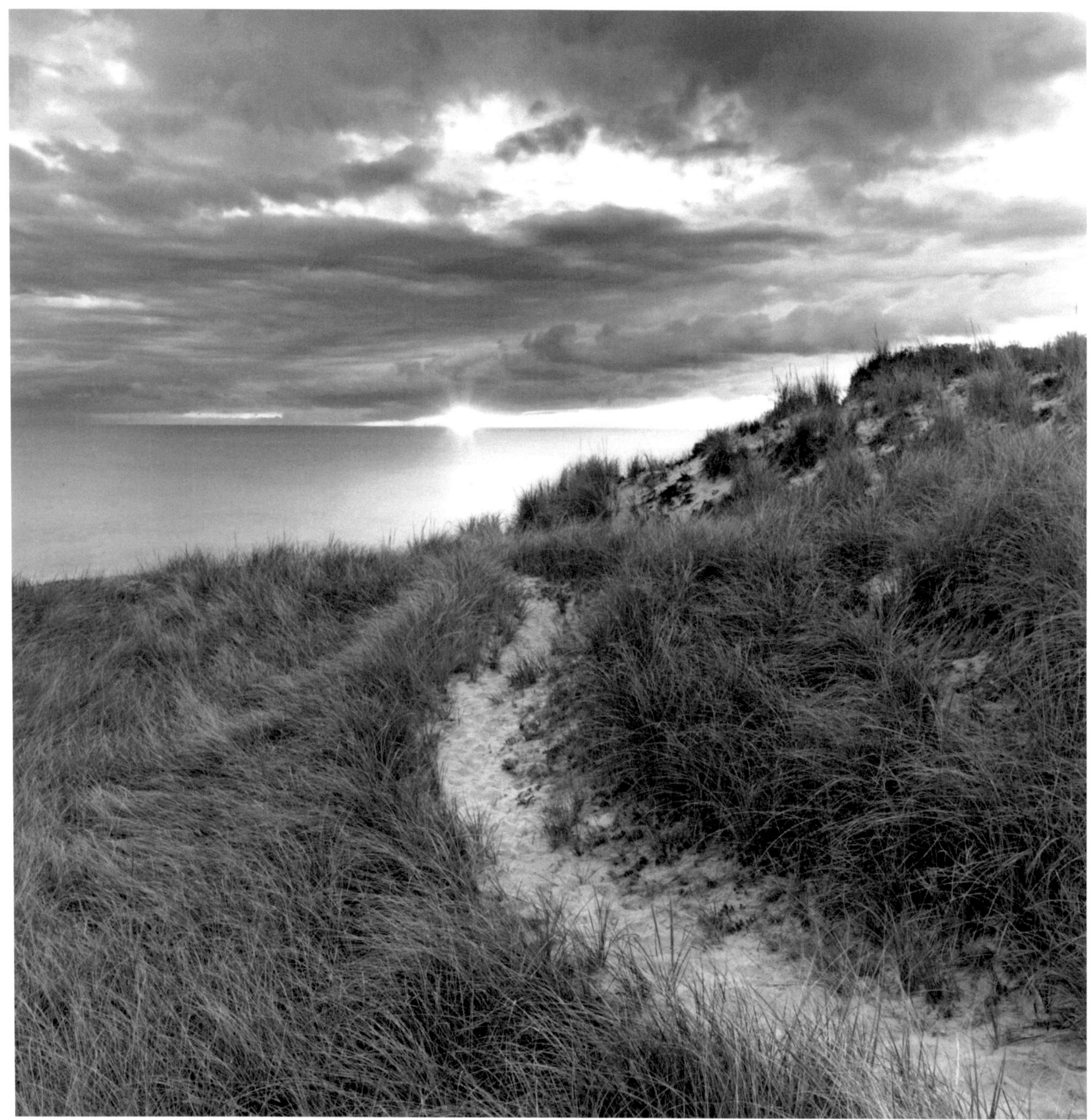

Martha's Vineyard, Massachusetts, 2017

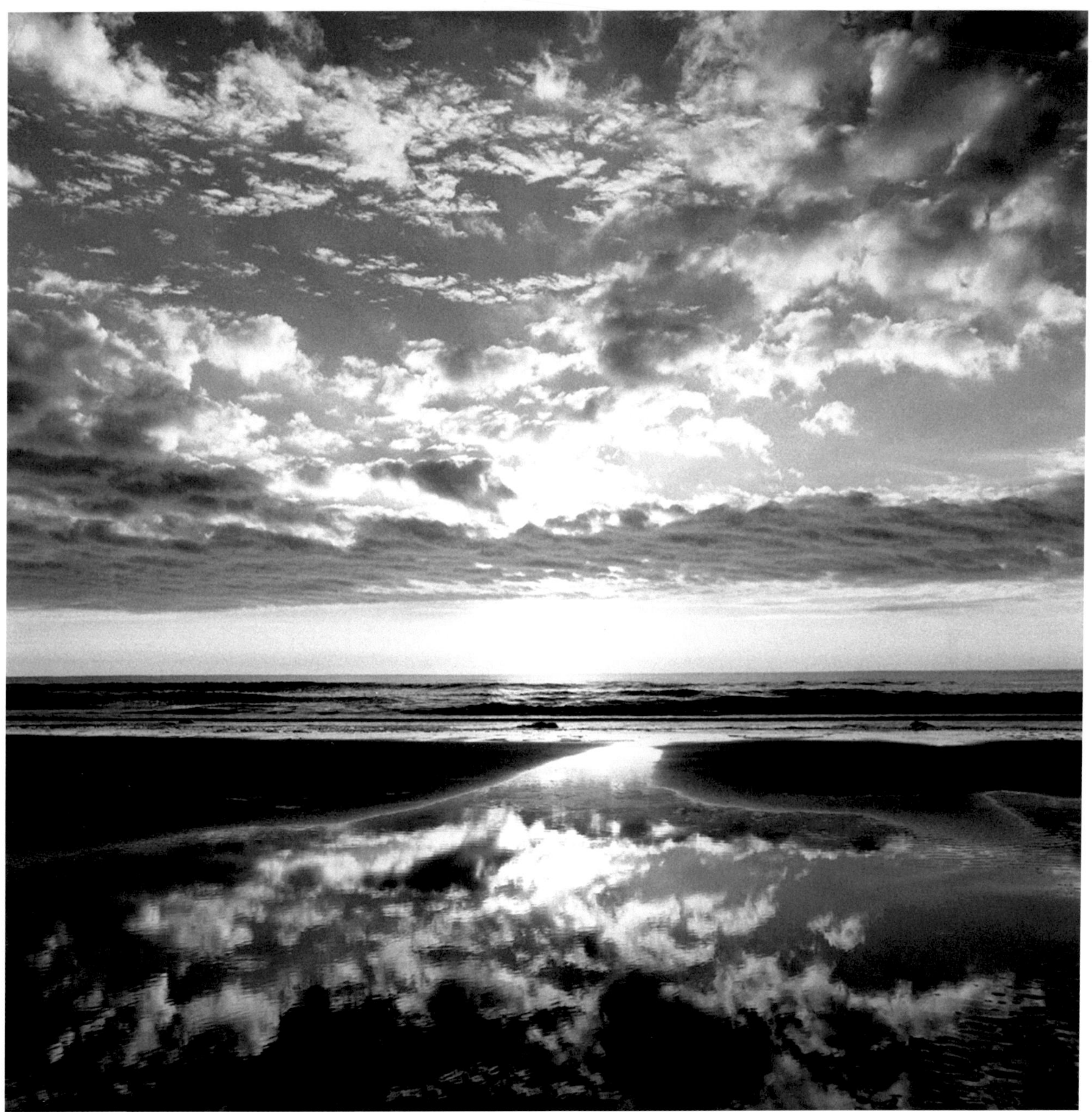

Topsail Beach, North Carolina, 2007

When anxious, uneasy, and bad thoughts come, I go to the sea, and the sea drowns them out with its great wide sounds, cleanses me with its noise, and imposes a rhythm upon everything in me that is bewildered and confused.

—RAINER MARIA RILKE

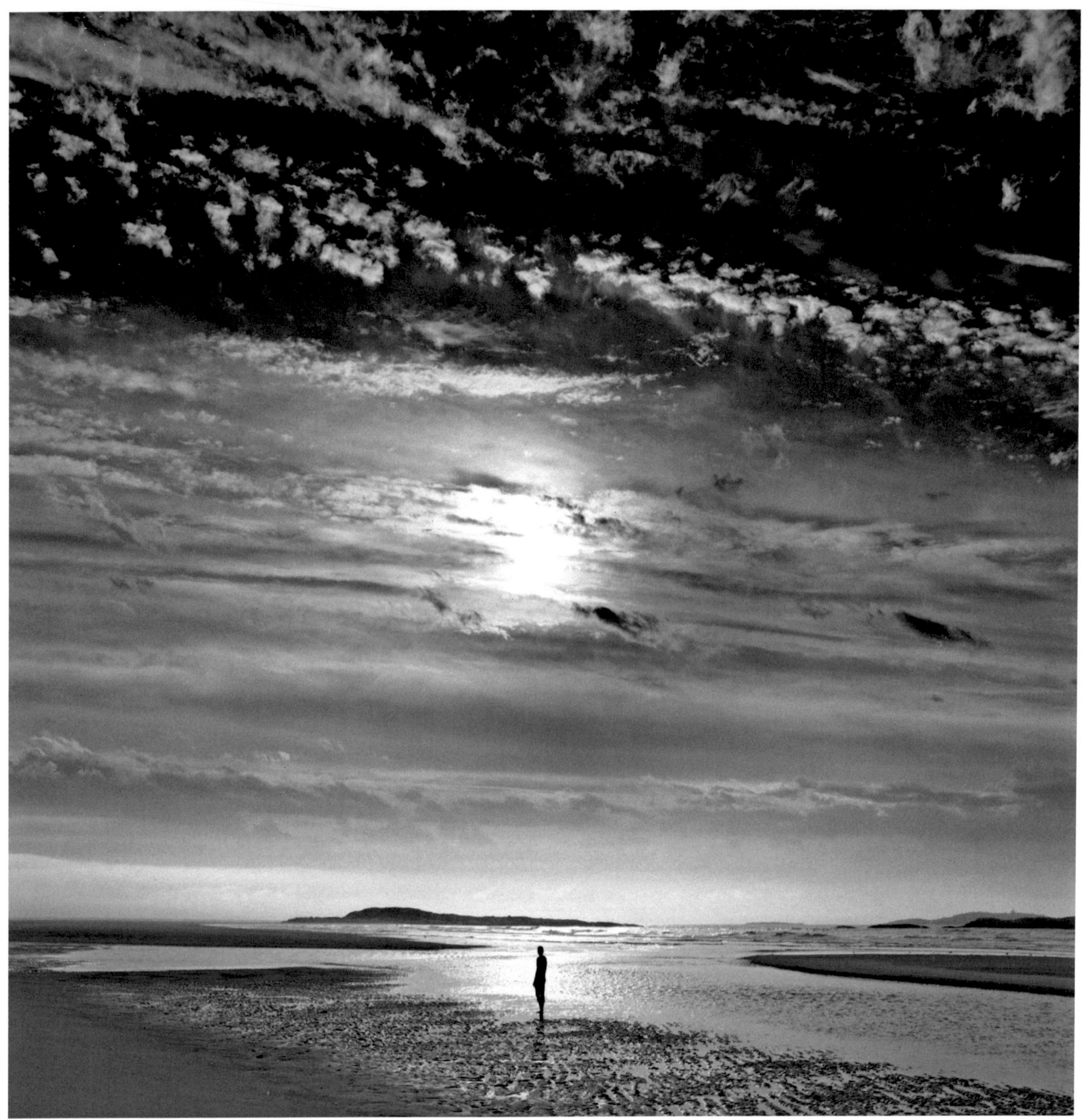

Popham Beach State Park, Maine, 2012

Martha's Vineyard, Massachusetts, 1999

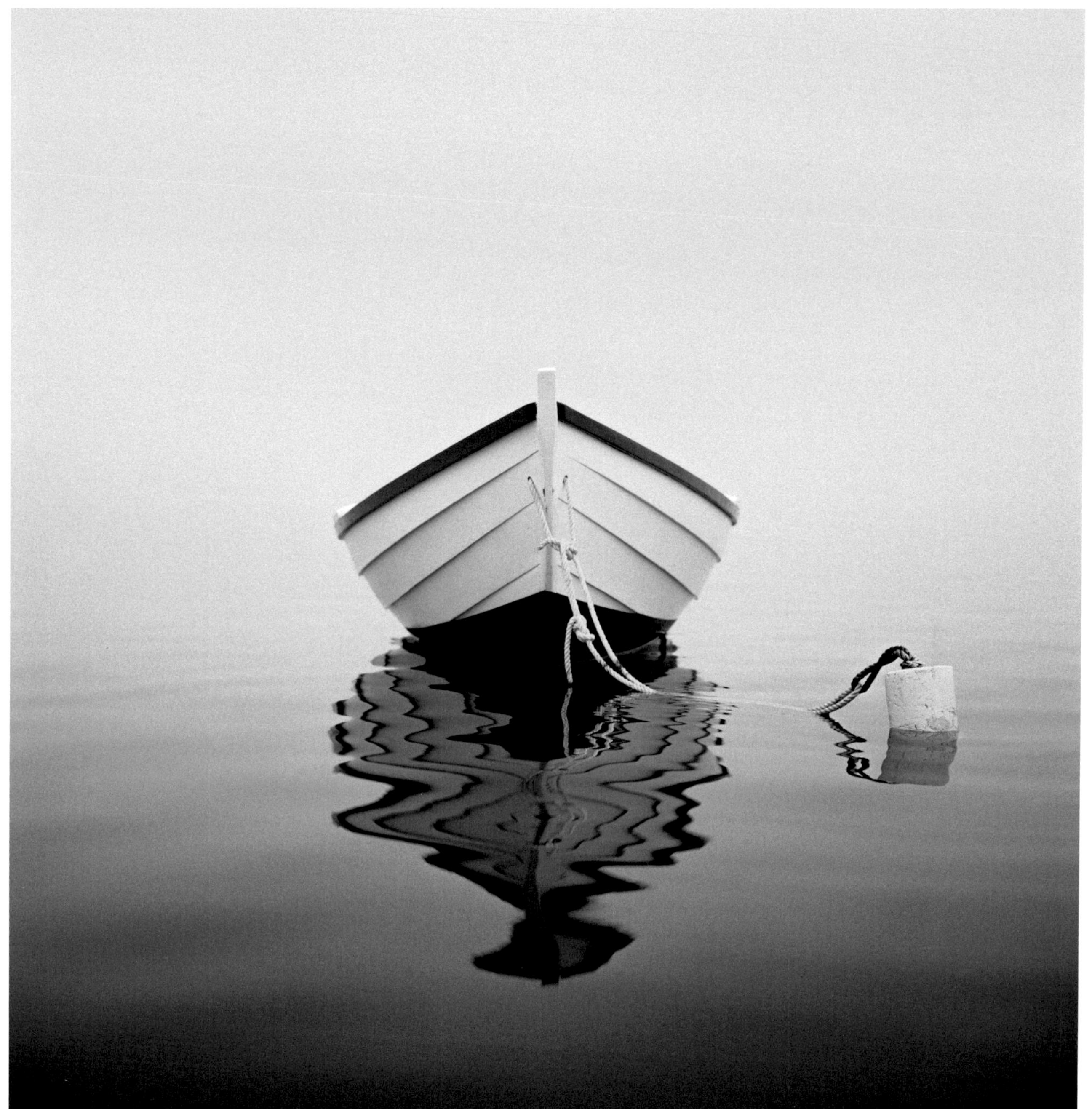

WoodenBoat School, Brooklin, Maine, 2018

*You are not a drop
in the ocean.
You are the entire ocean
in a drop.*

———————————

—RUMI

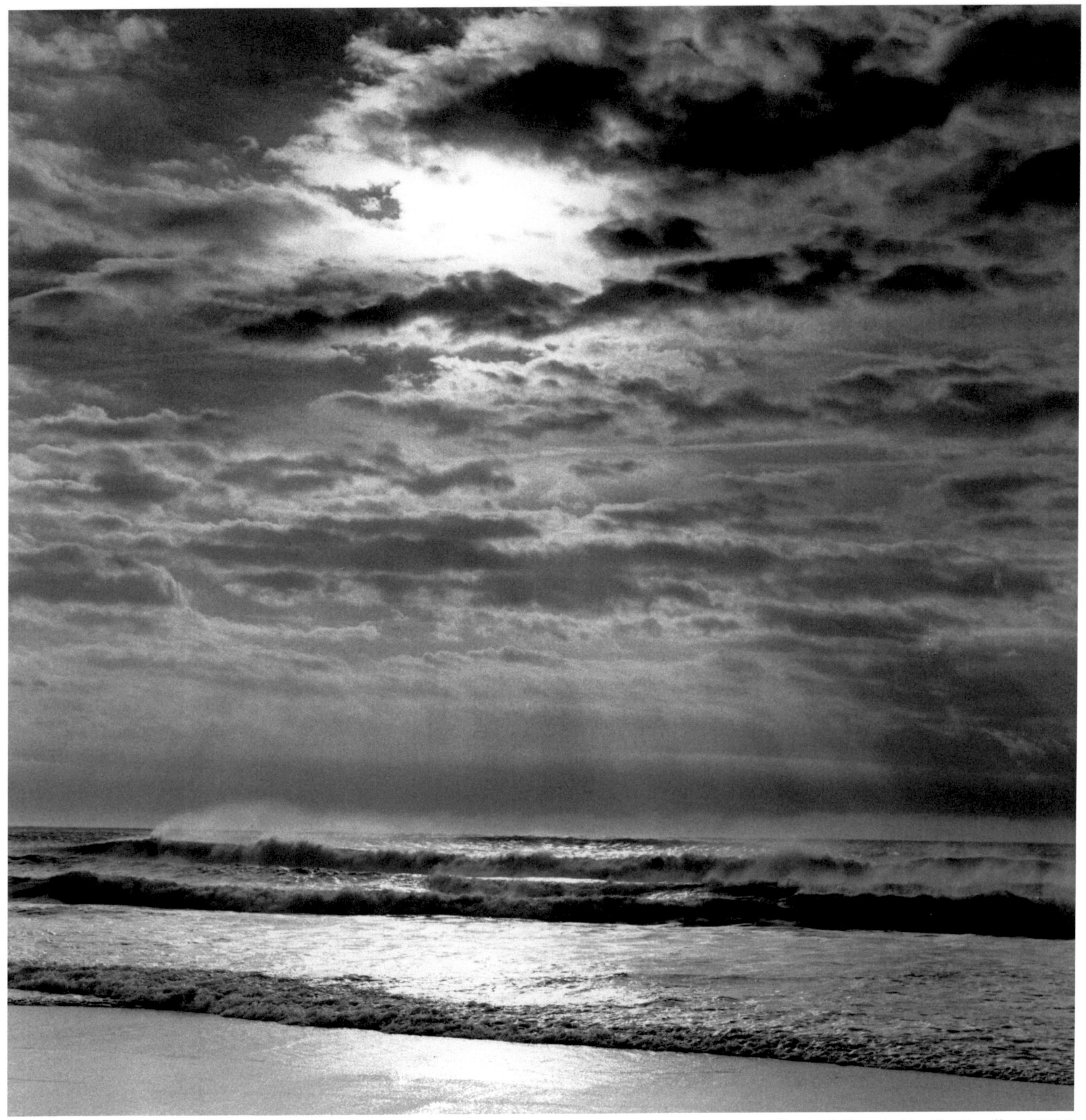

Topsail Beach, North Carolina, 2008

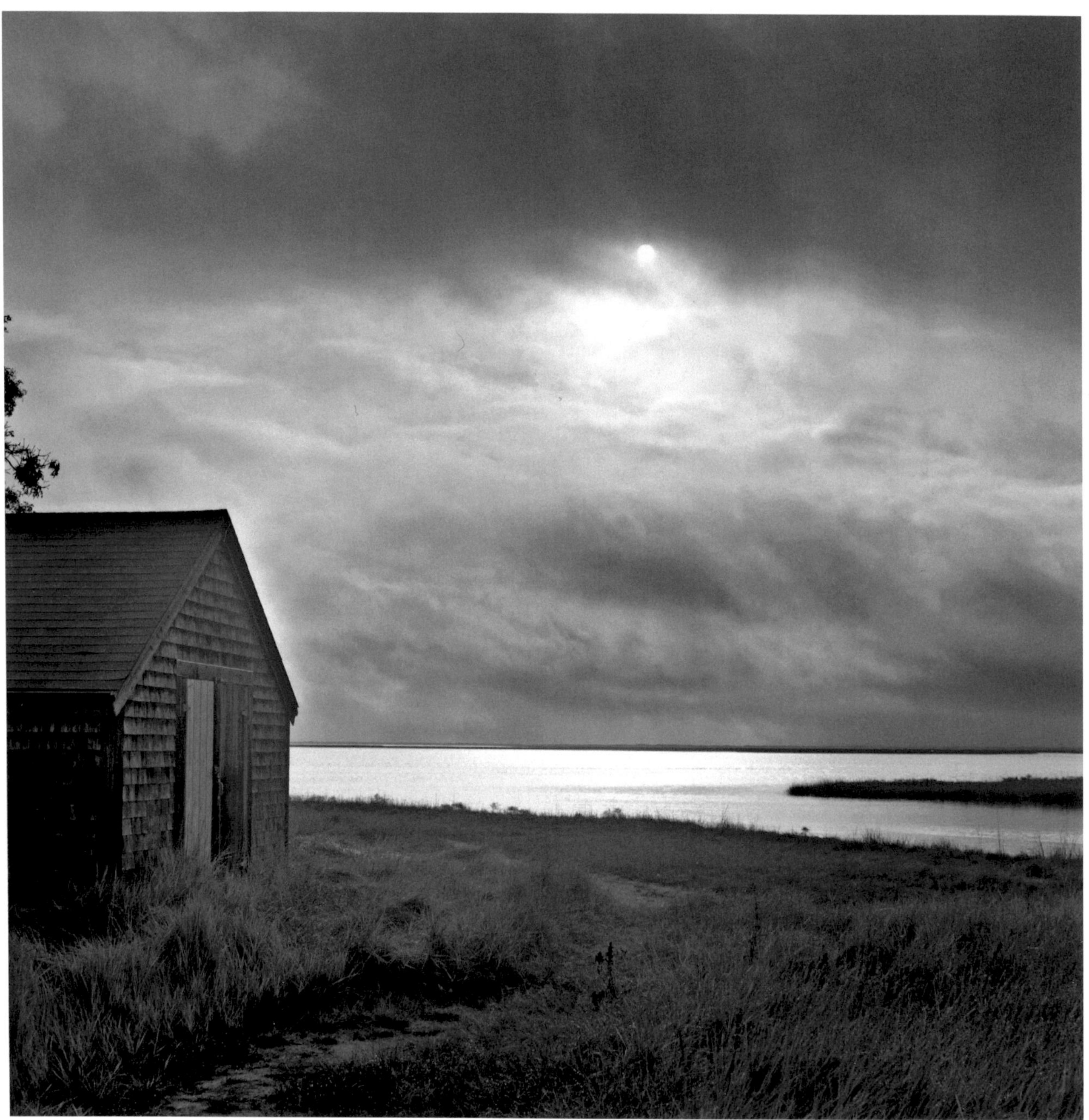

Cape Cod National Seashore, Massachusetts, 2015

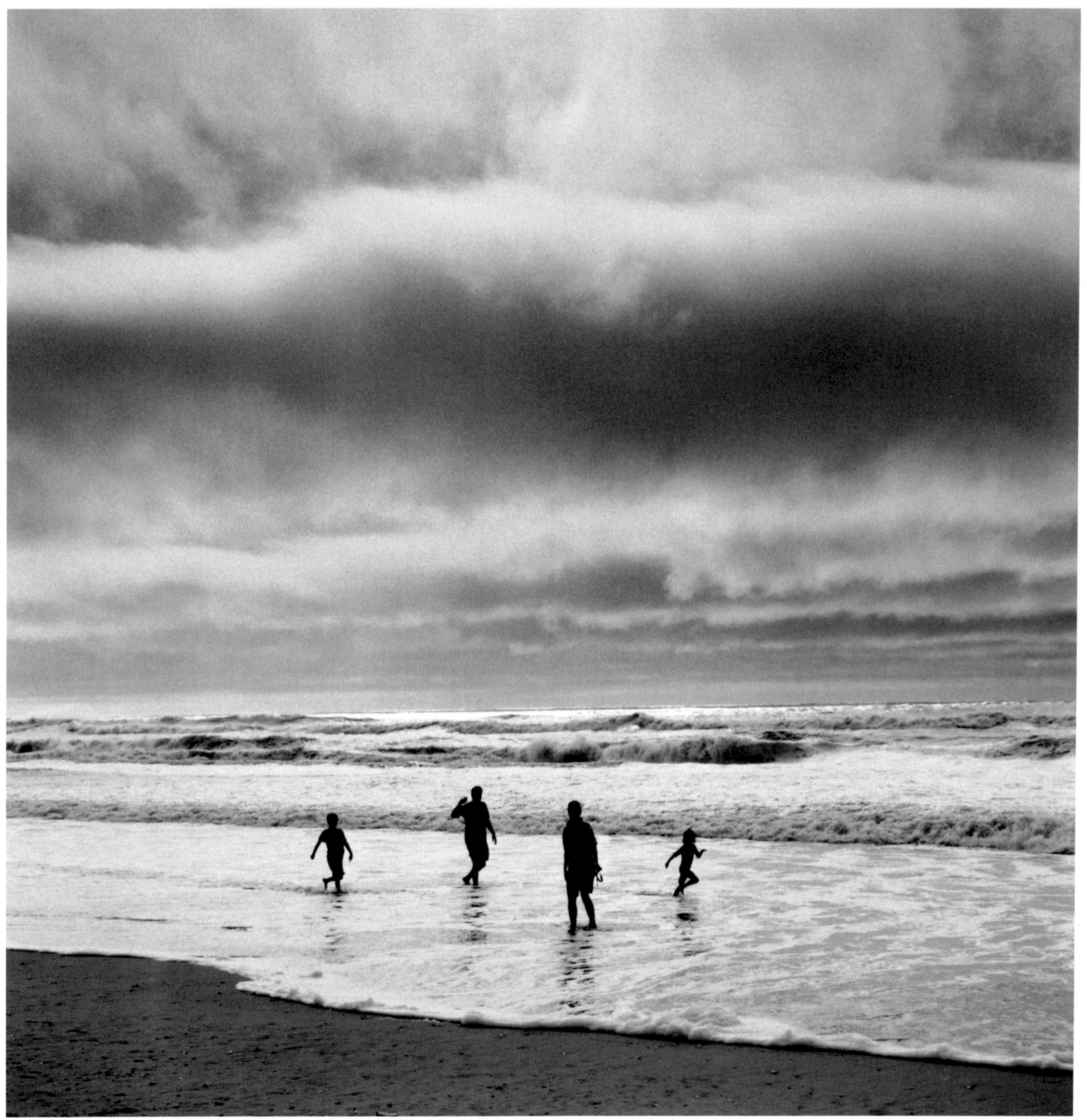

Topsail Beach, North Carolina, 2007

*The softest things in the world
overcome the hardest things in
the world.*

—LAO TZU

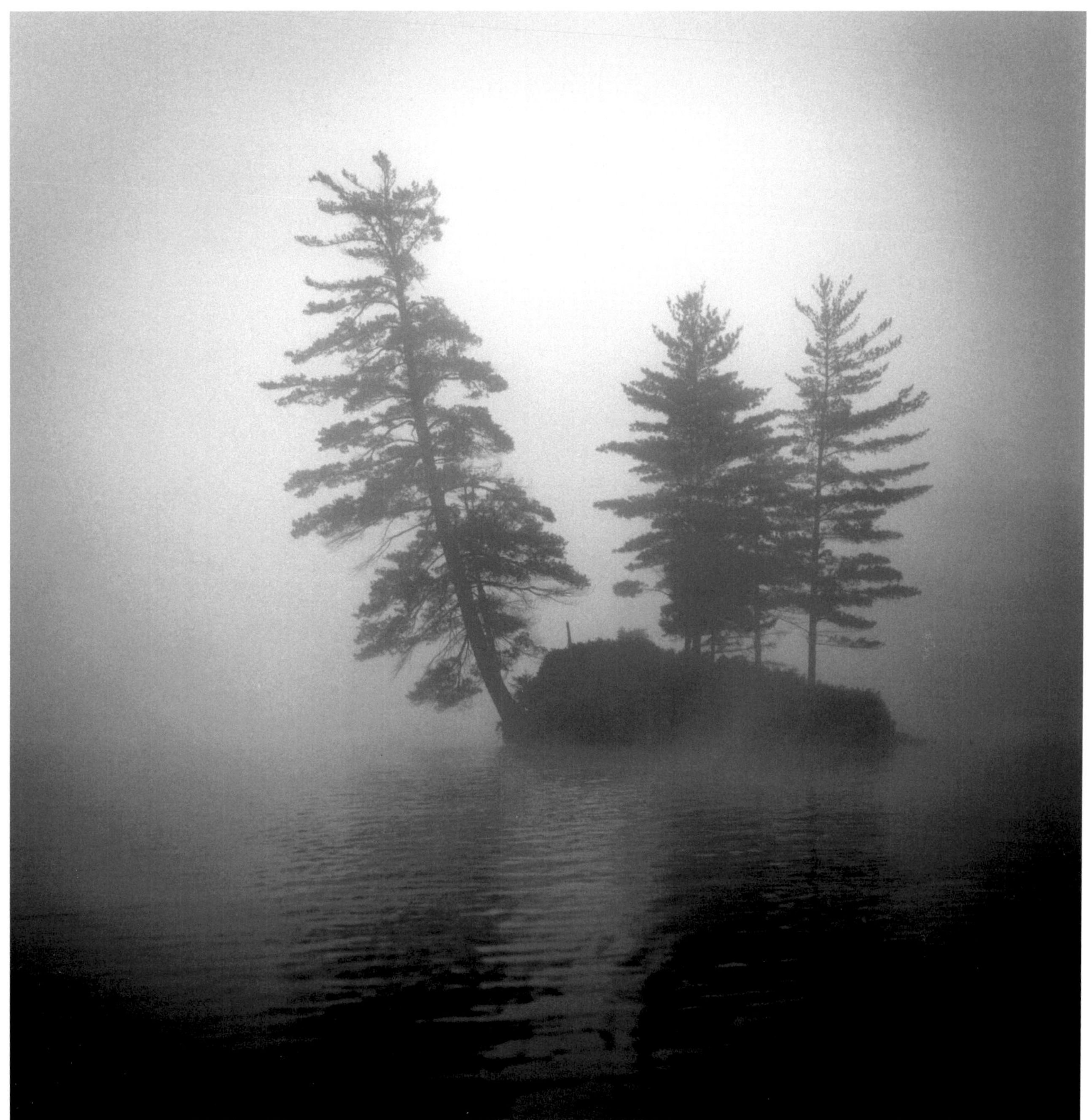

Adirondacks, New York, 2002

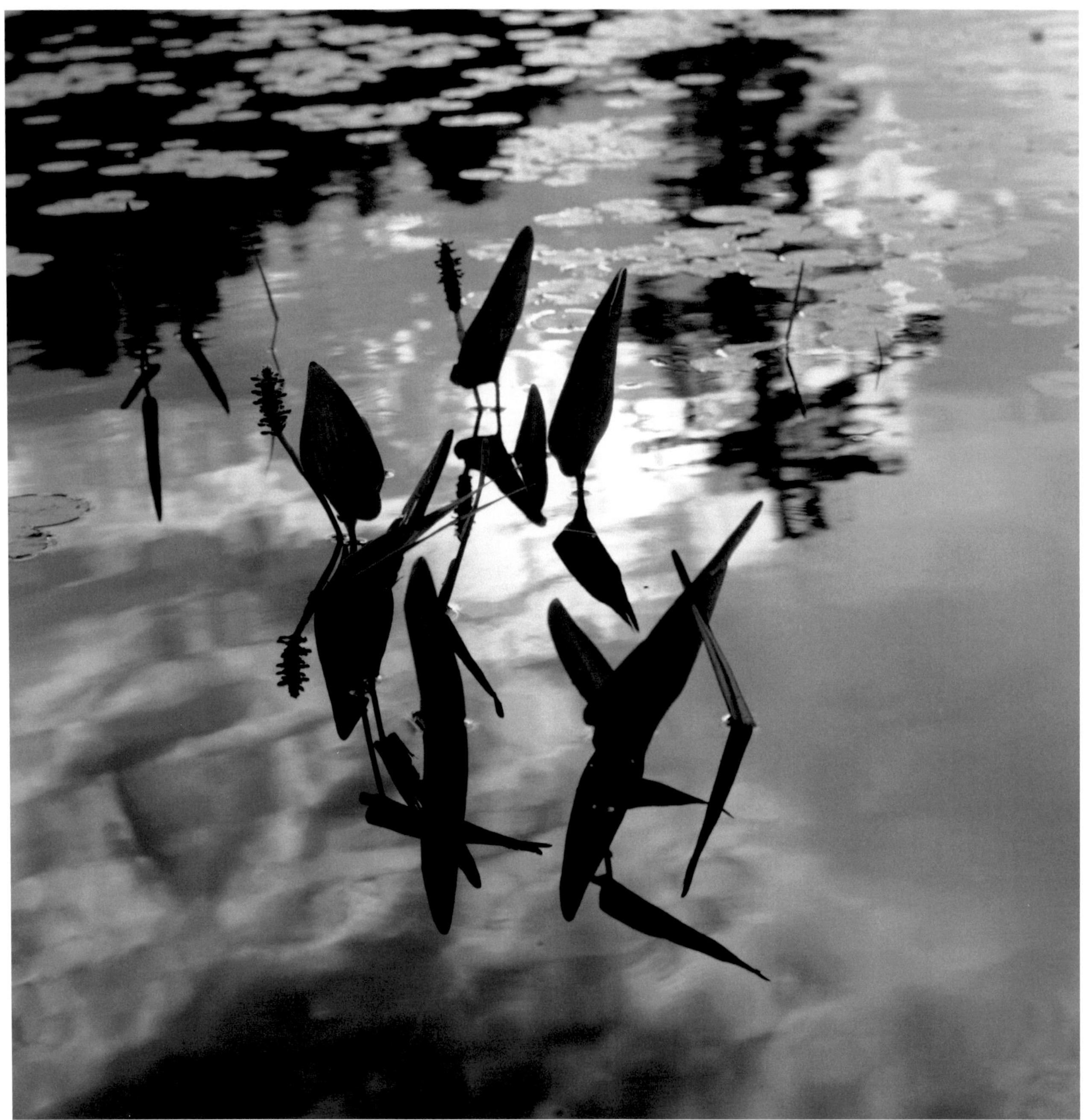

St. Regis Lake, New York, 2012

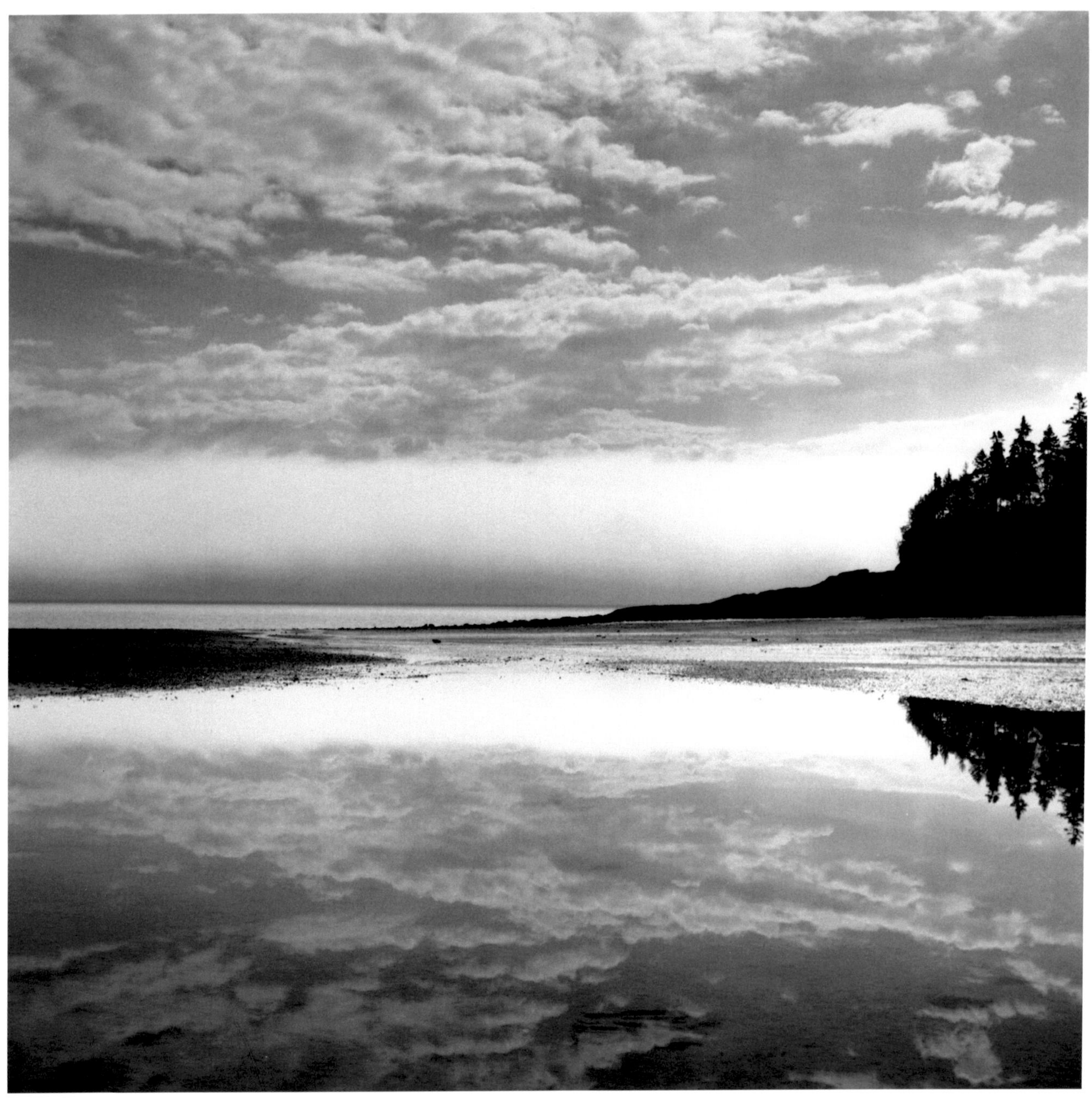

Bay of Fundy National Park, New Brunswick, Canada, 2018

—How wild it was to let it be.

———————————————————

—CHERYL STRAYED

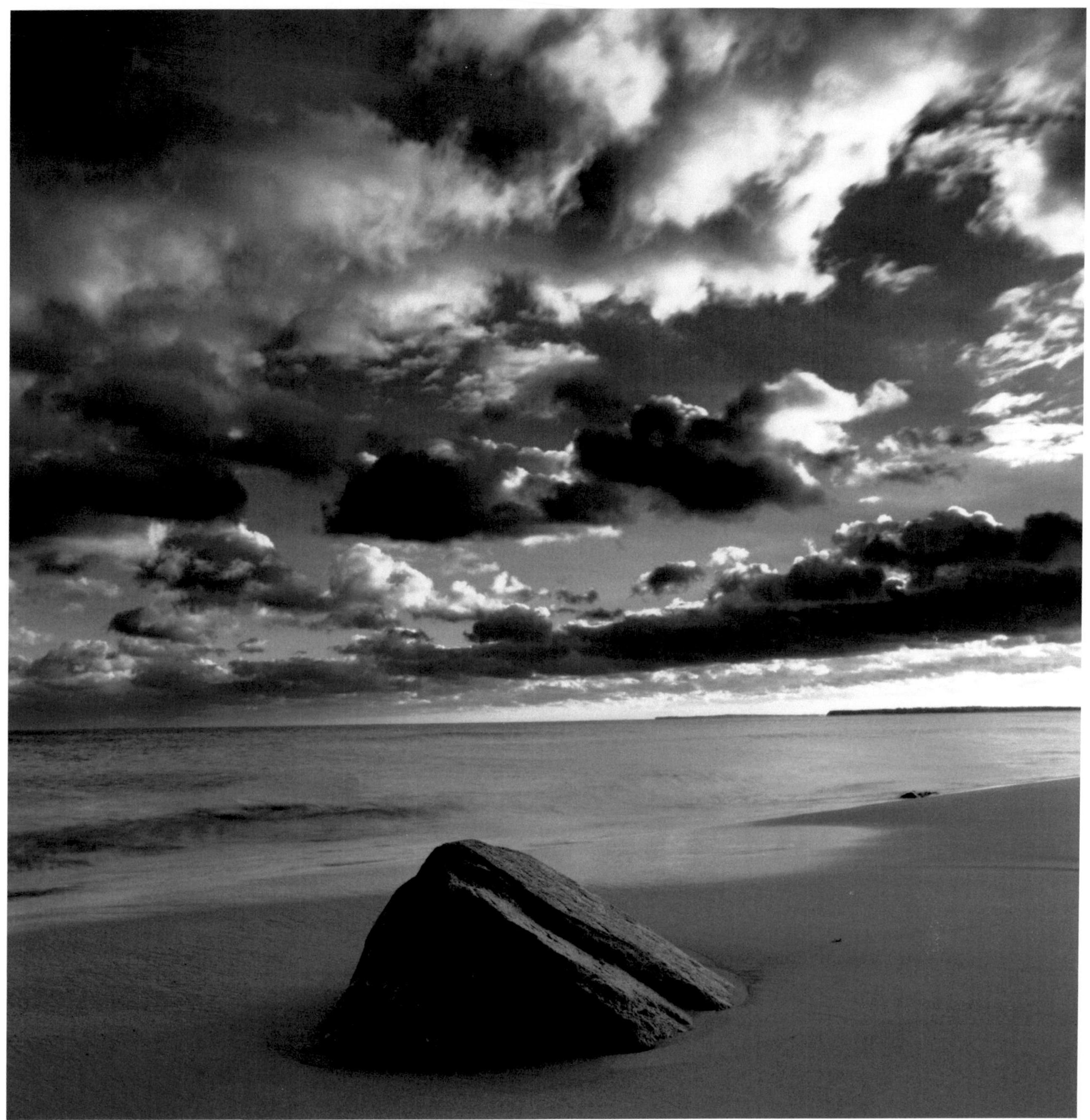

Martha's Vineyard, Massachusetts, 1999

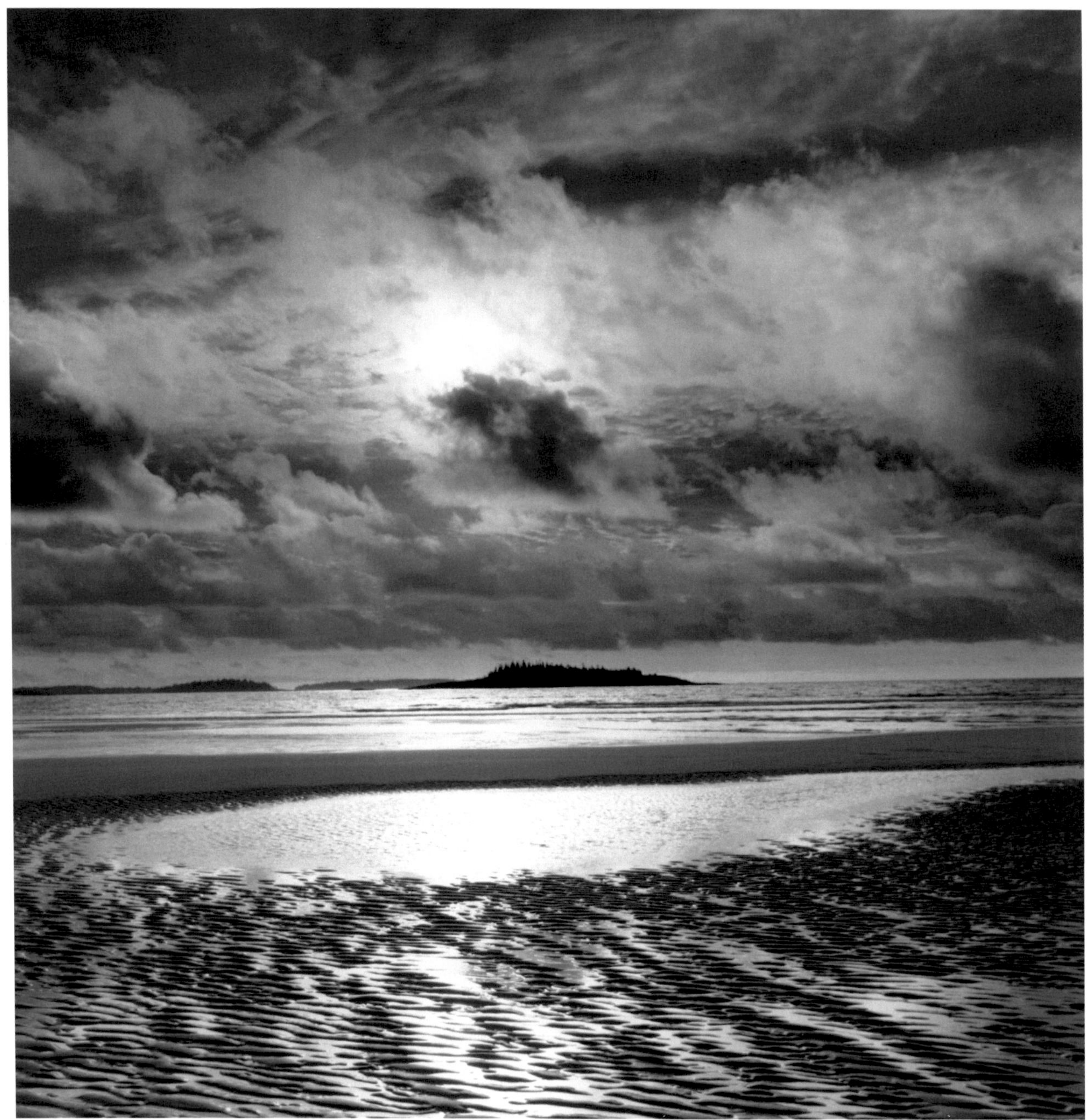

Popham Beach State Park, Maine, 2018

Martha's Vineyard, Massachusetts, 2011

*Don't move the way fear makes
you move. Move the way love
makes you move. Move the
way joy makes you move.*

———————————

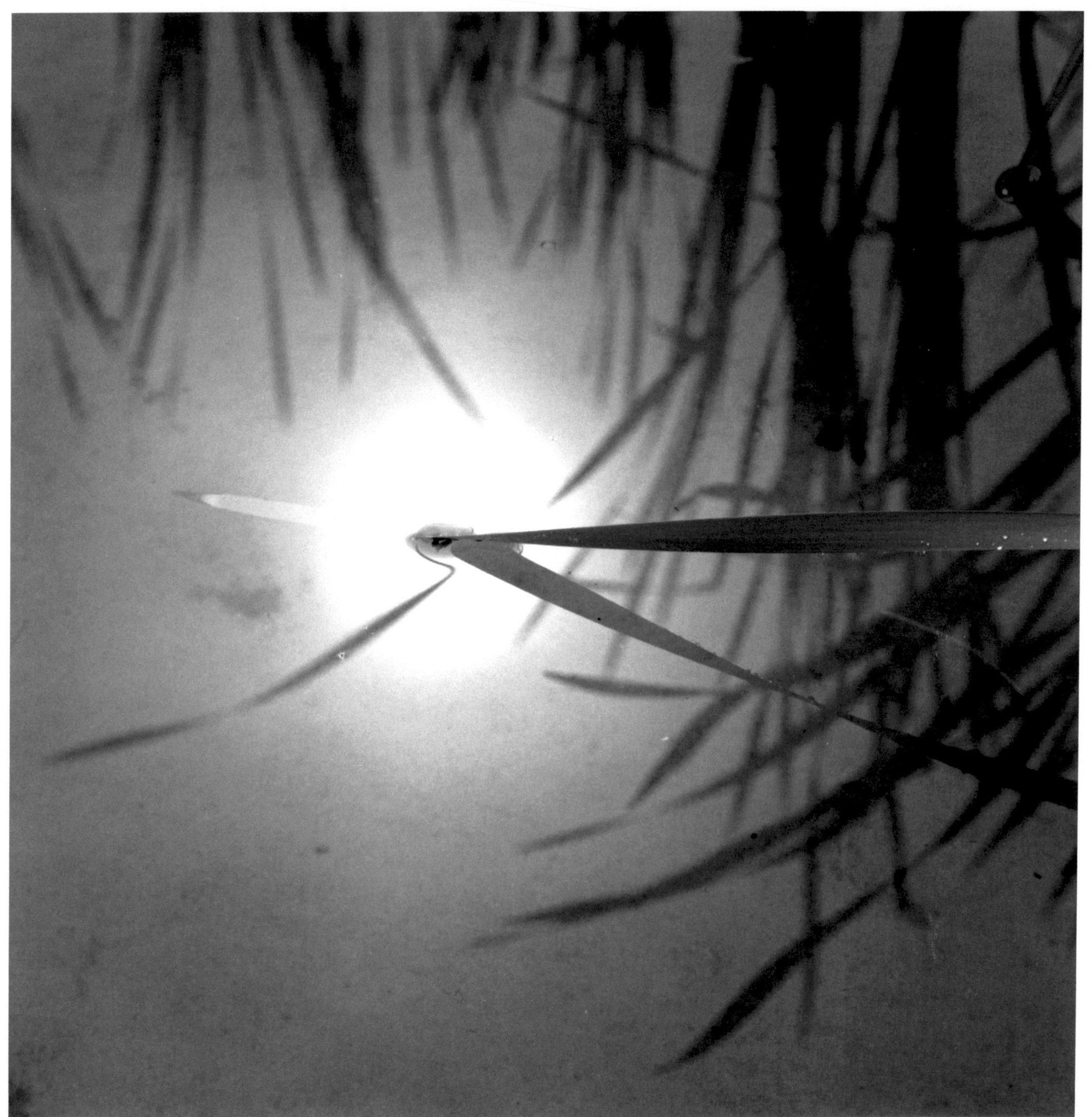

Nickerson State Park, Cape Cod, Massachusetts, 2015

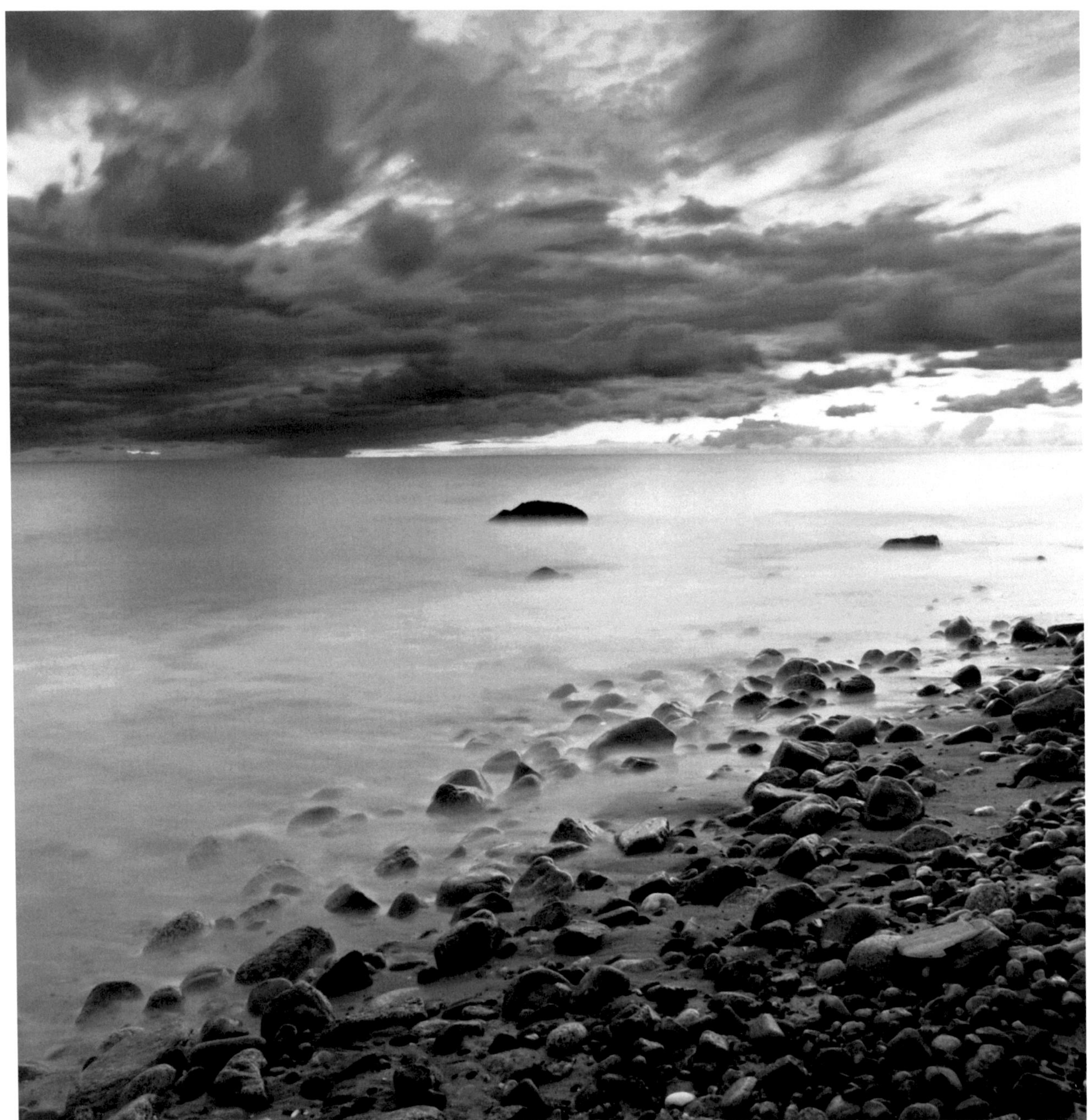

Martha's Vineyard, Massachusetts, 2017

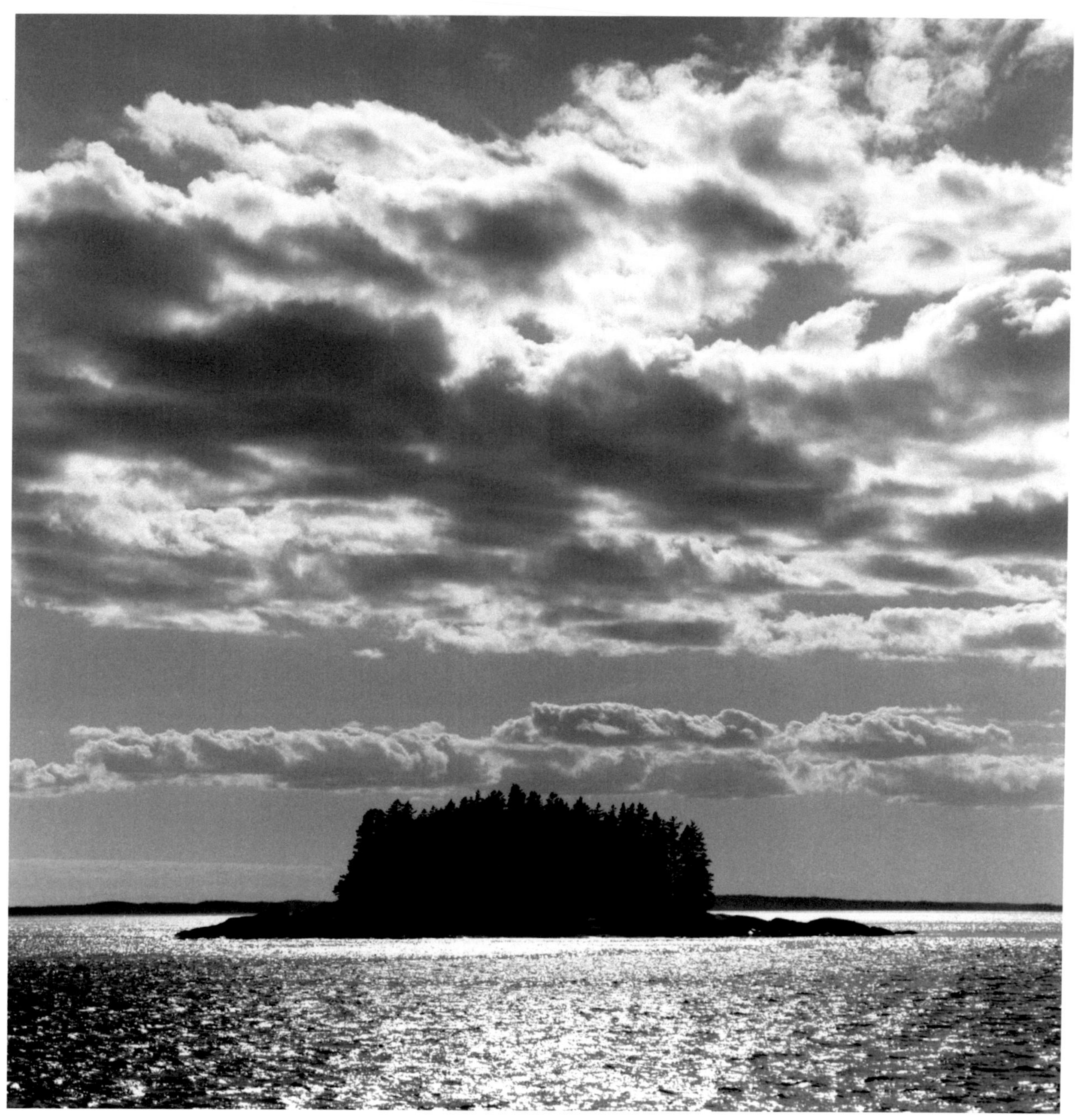

Penobscot Bay, Maine, 2010

*My soul is full of longing
for the secrets of the sea,
and the heart of the great ocean
sends a thrilling pulse through me.*

—HENRY WADSWORTH LONGFELLOW

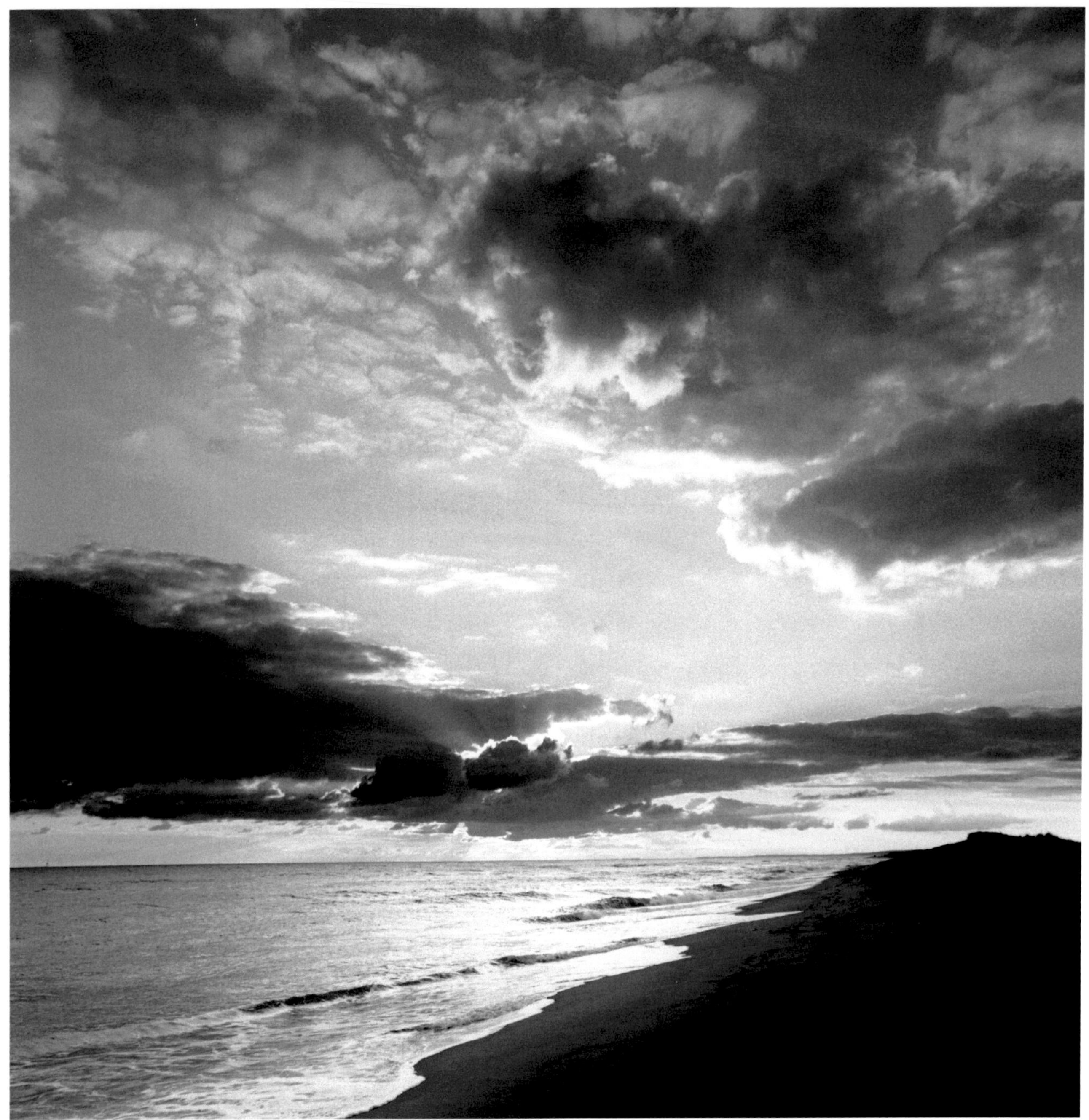

Martha's Vineyard, Massachusetts, 2006

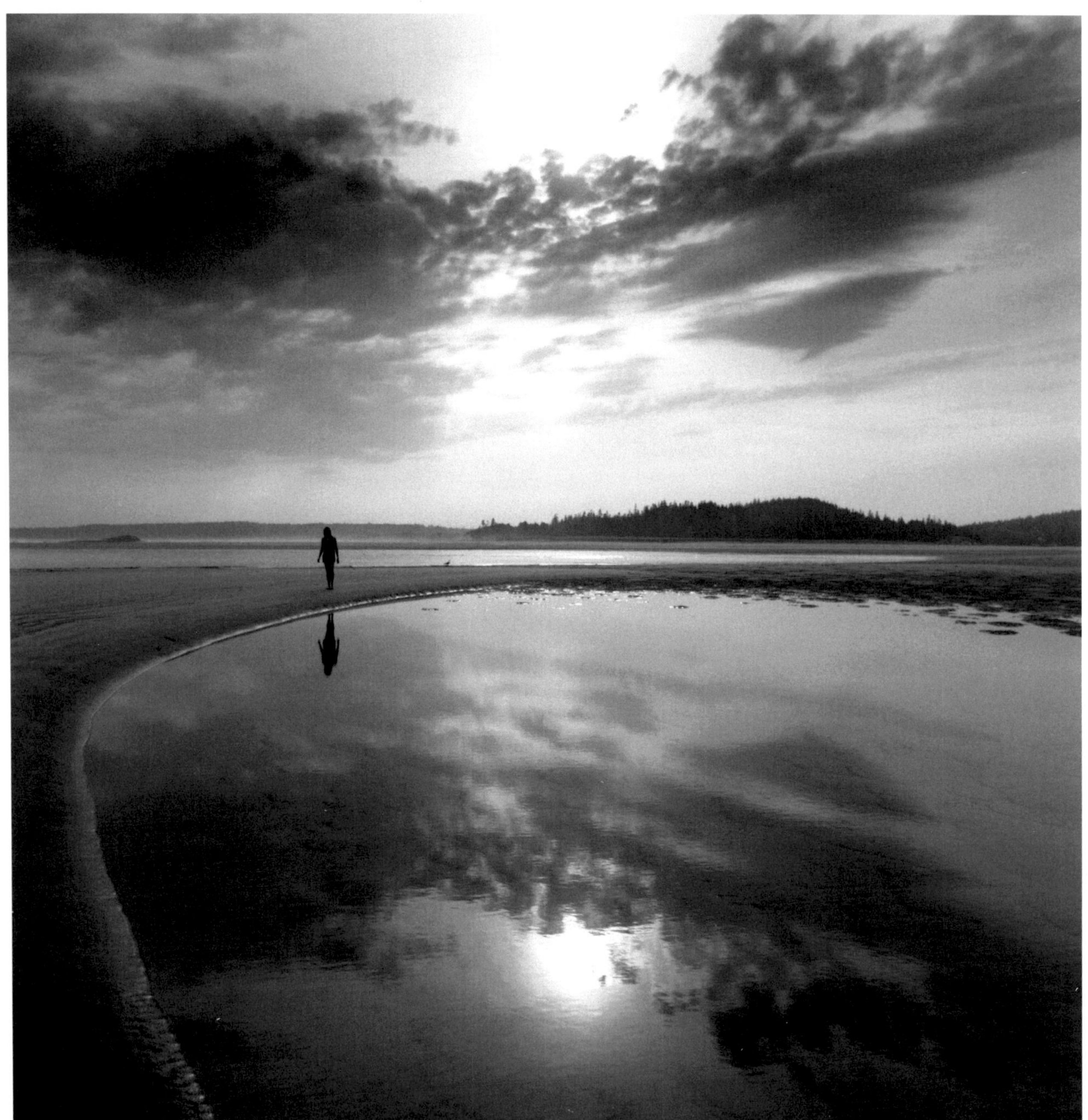

Popham Beach State Park, Maine, 2011

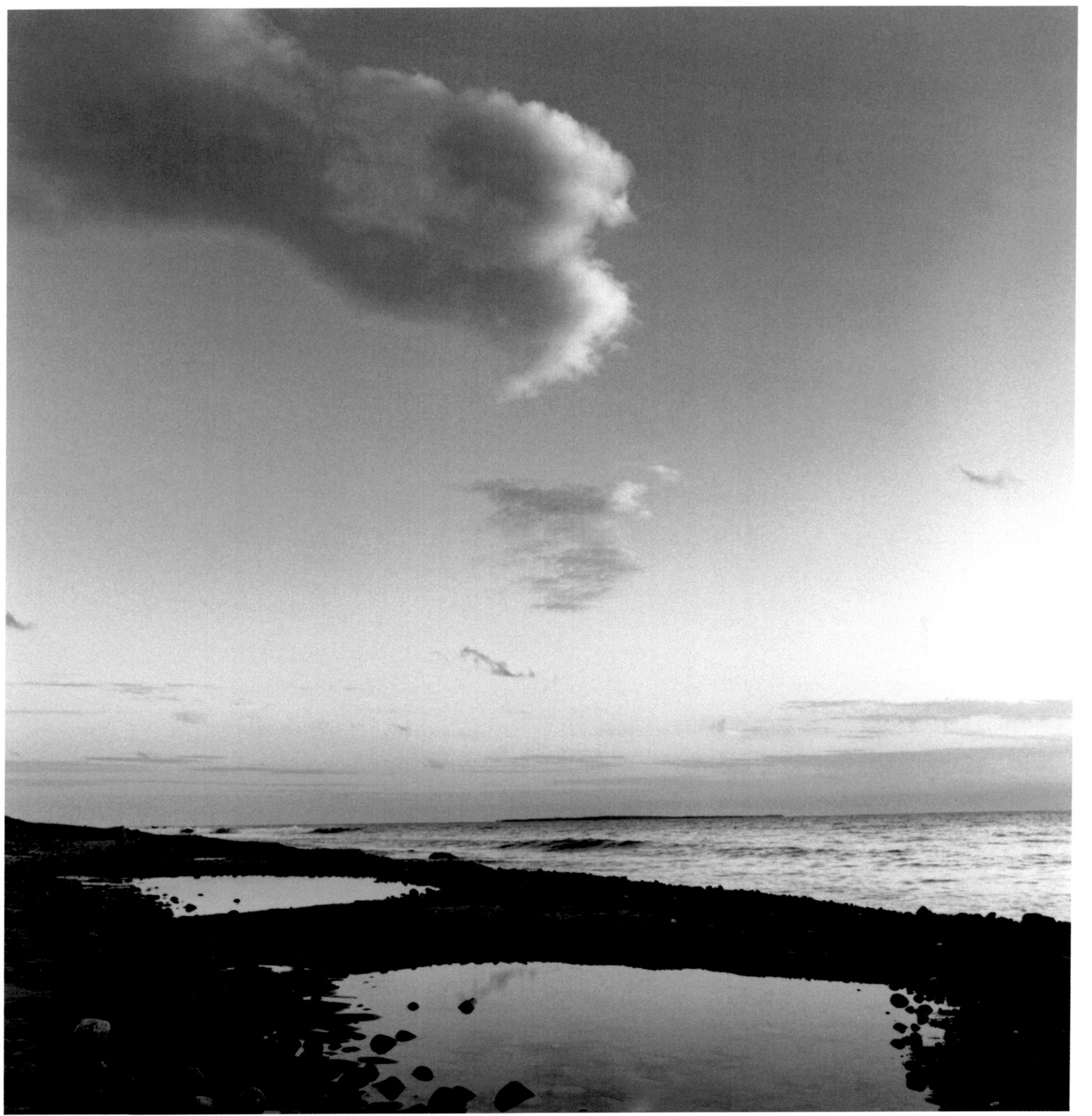

Martha's Vineyard, Massachusetts, 1999

*Every time I stand before a beautiful
beach, its waves seem to whisper to me:
if you choose the simple things and
find joy in nature's simple treasures,
life and living need not be so hard.*

—PSYCHE ROXAS-MENDOZA

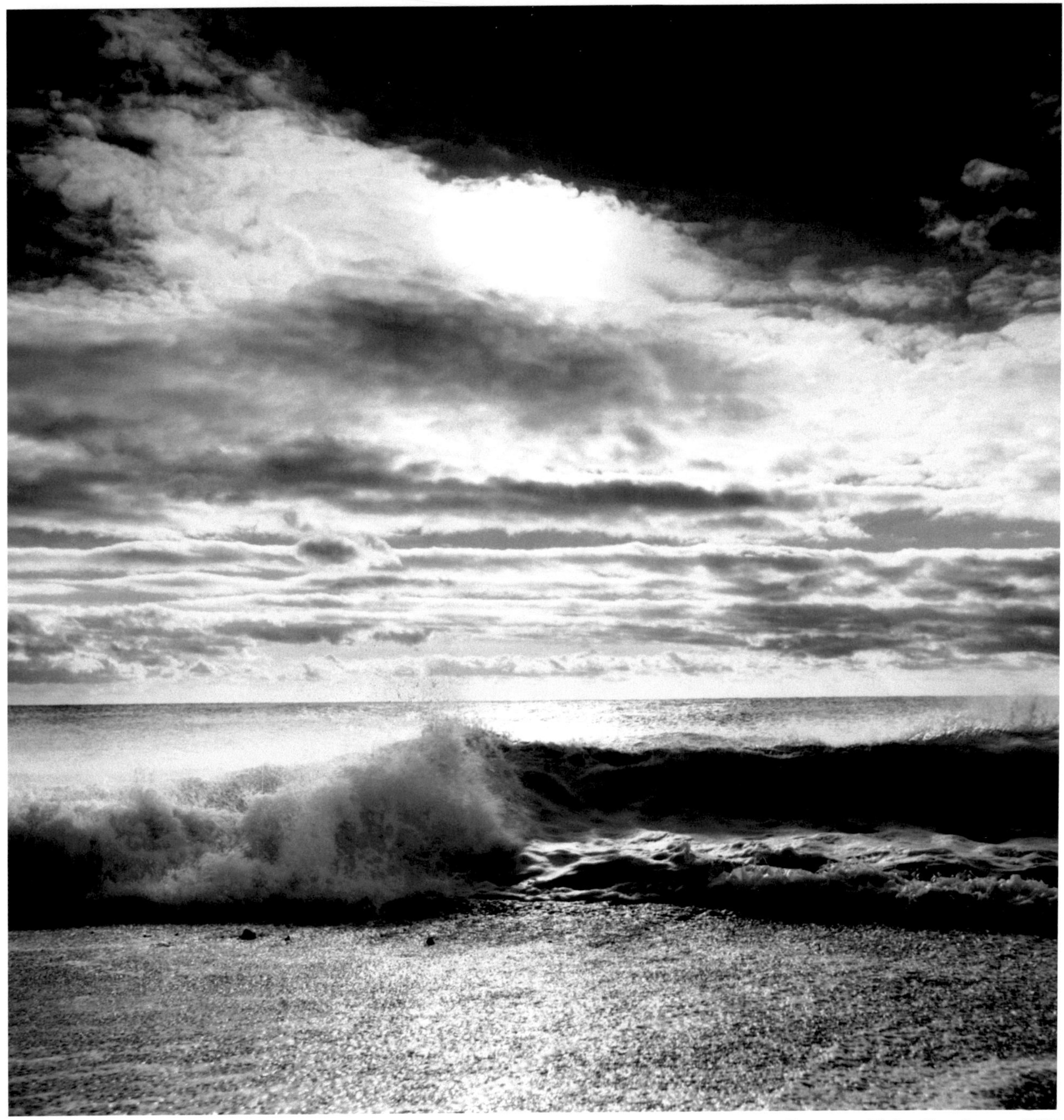

Barnegat Light, New Jersey, 2017

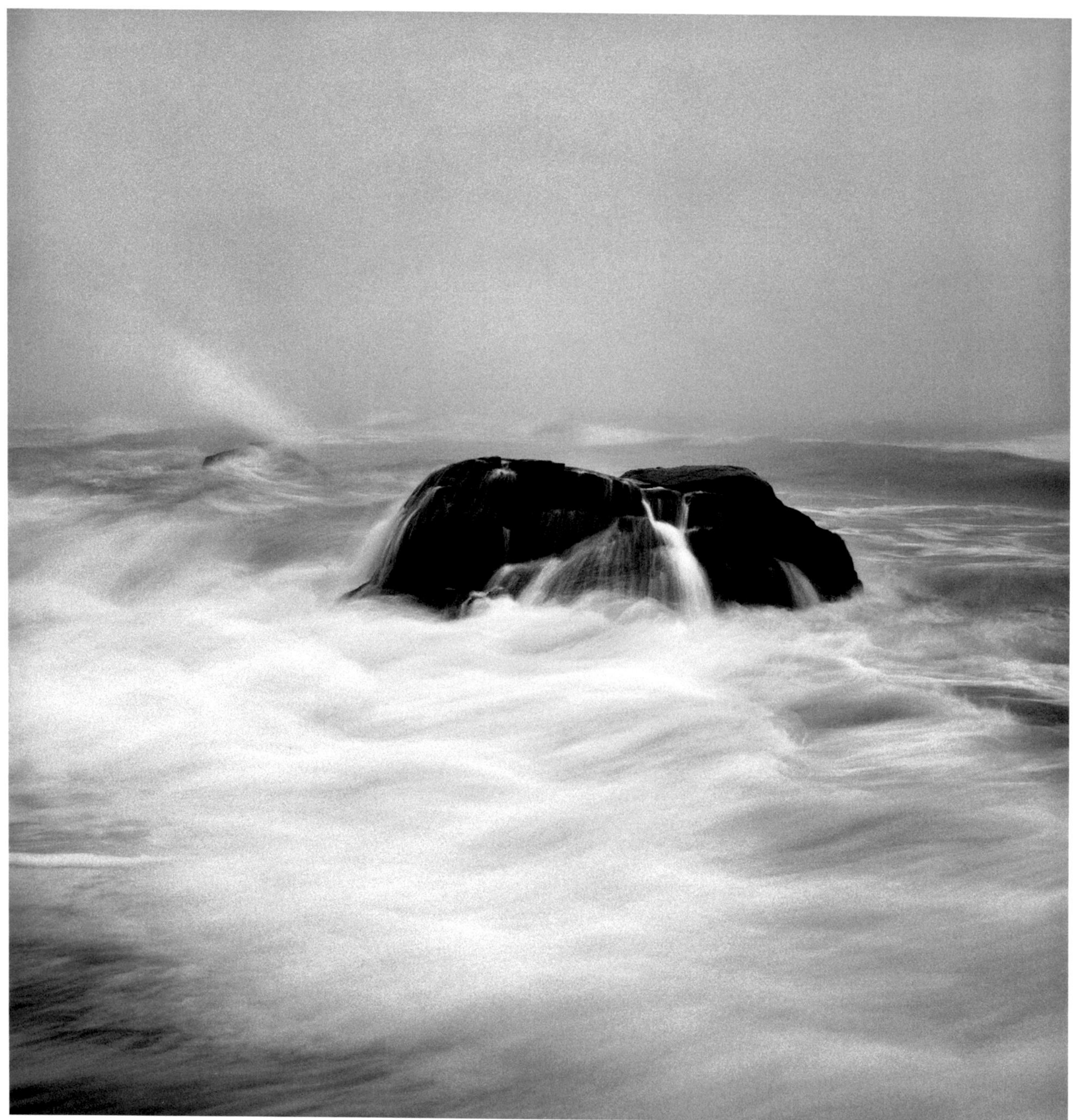

Martha's Vineyard, Massachusetts, 2004

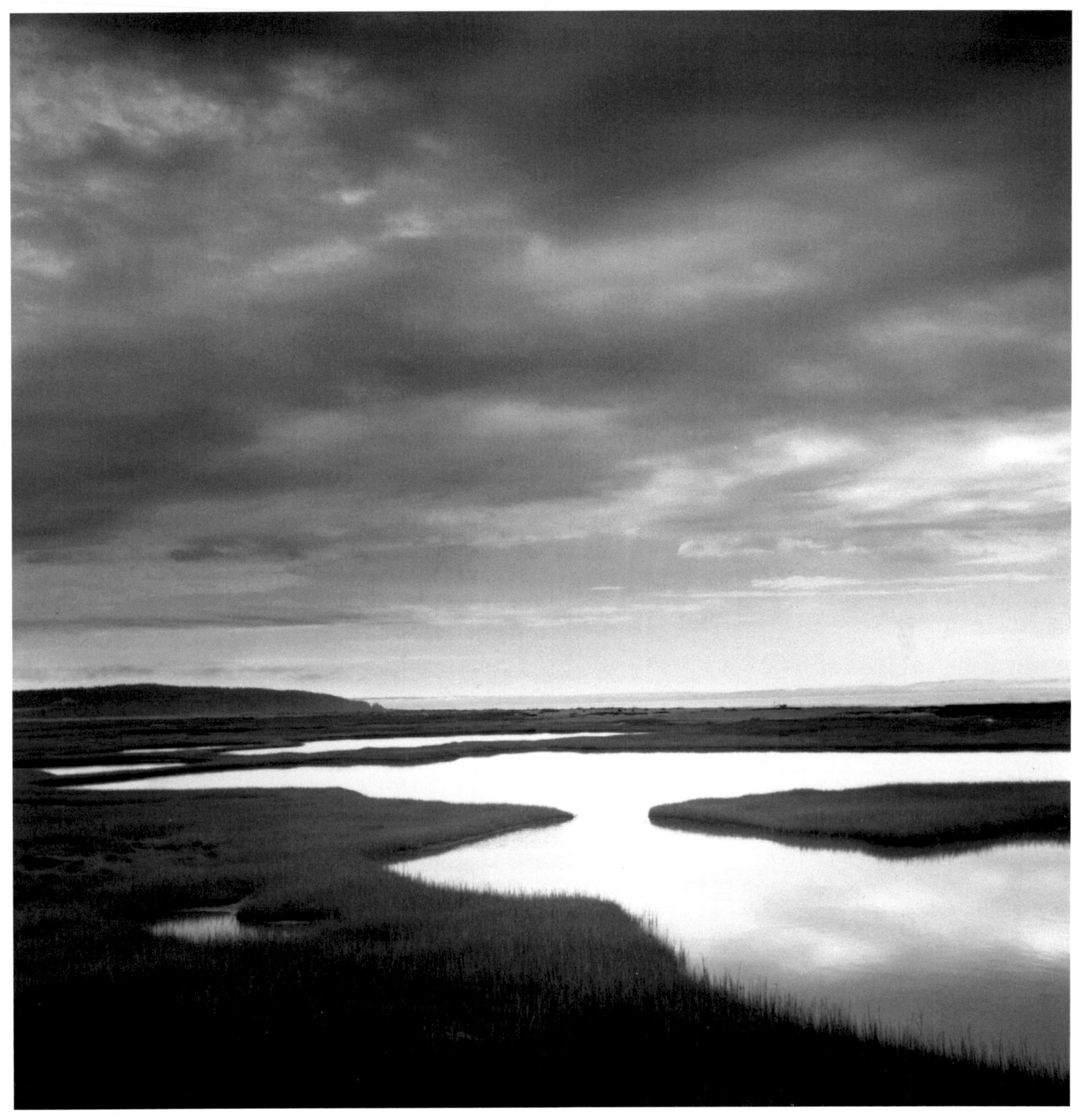

Bay of Fundy National Park, New Brunswick, Canada, 2018

The meaning of life is to just be alive. It is so plain and so obvious and so simple.

—ALAN WATTS

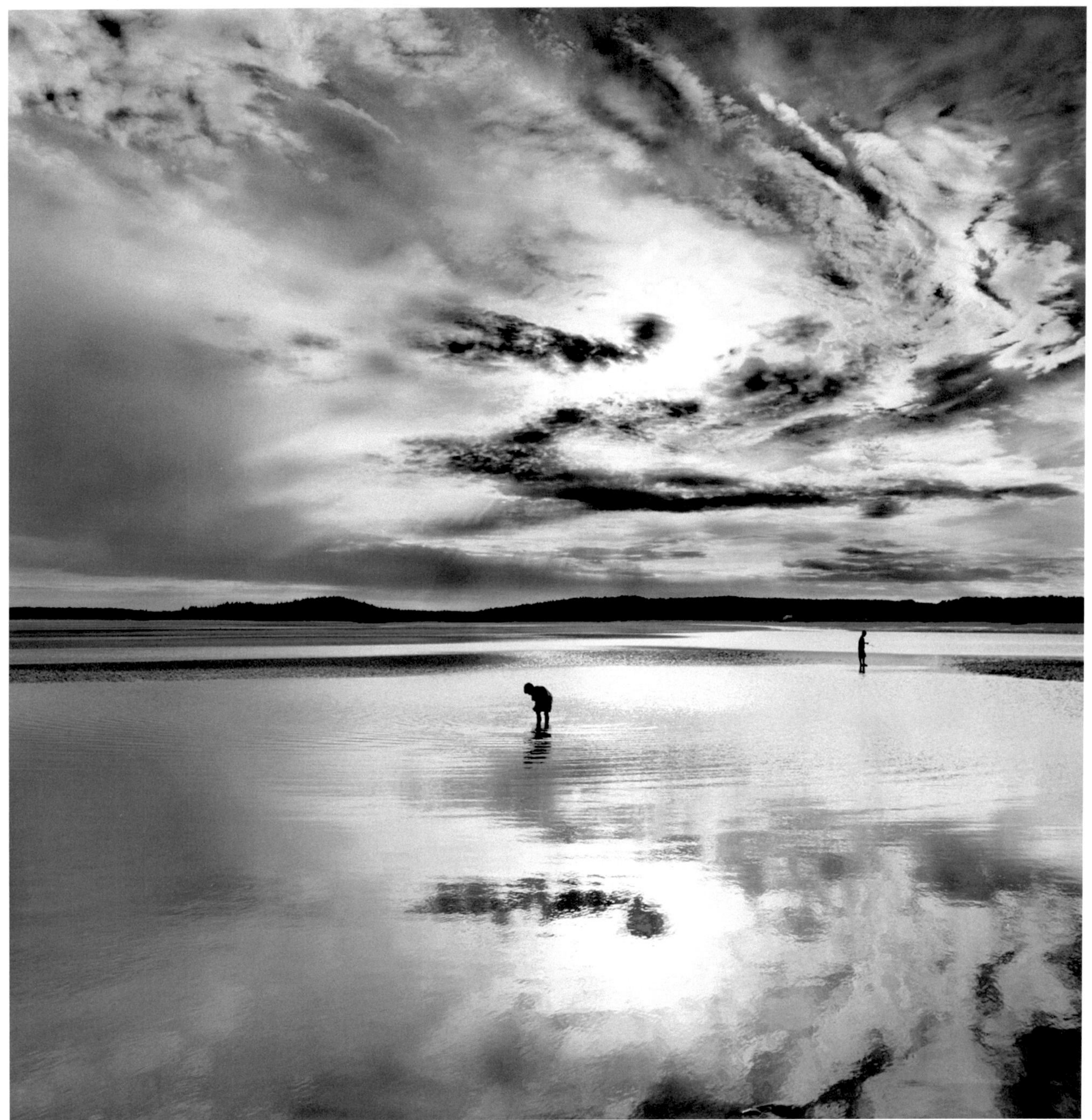

Popham Beach State Park, Maine, 2002

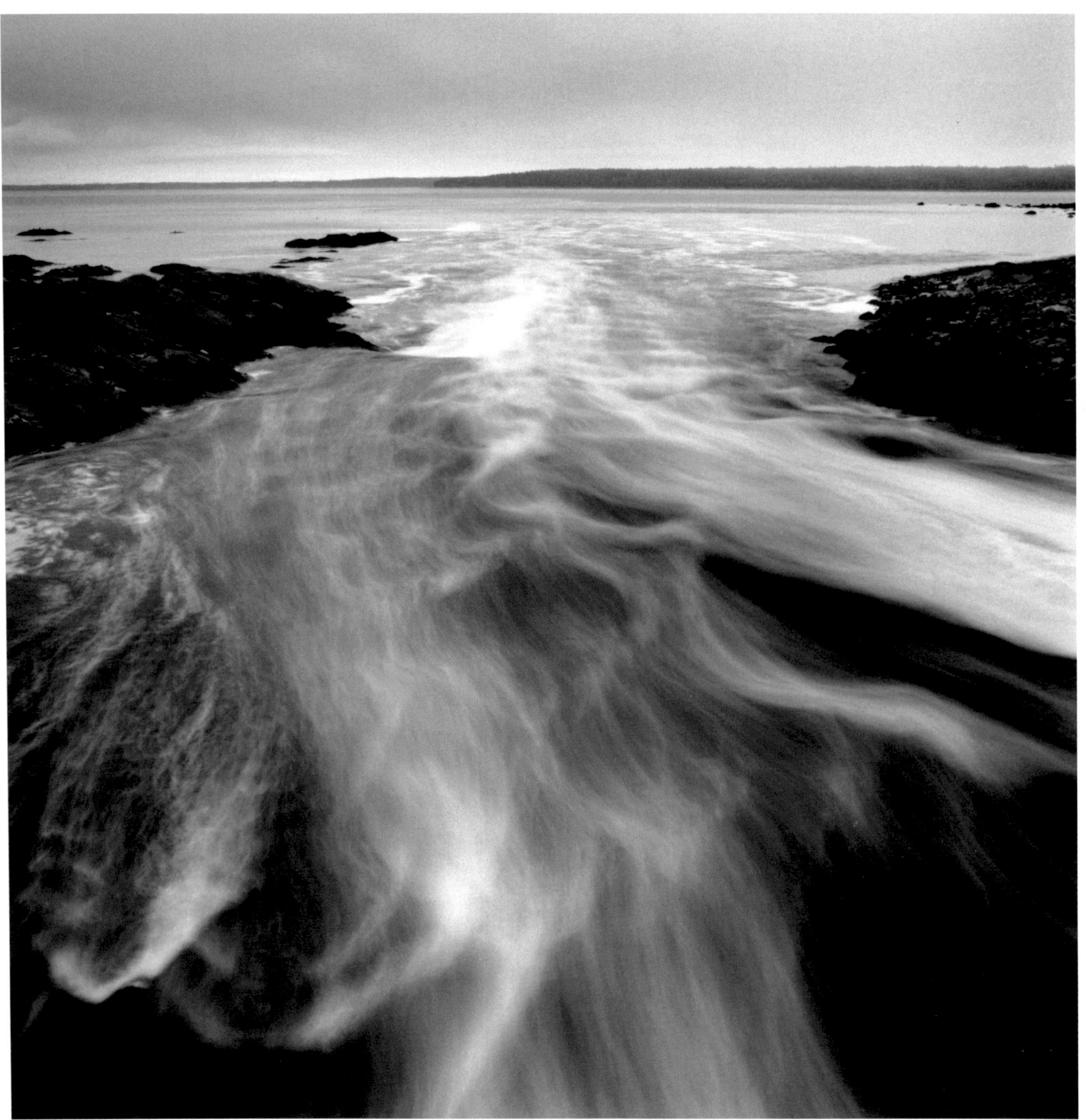

Blue Hill Reversing Falls, Maine, 2019

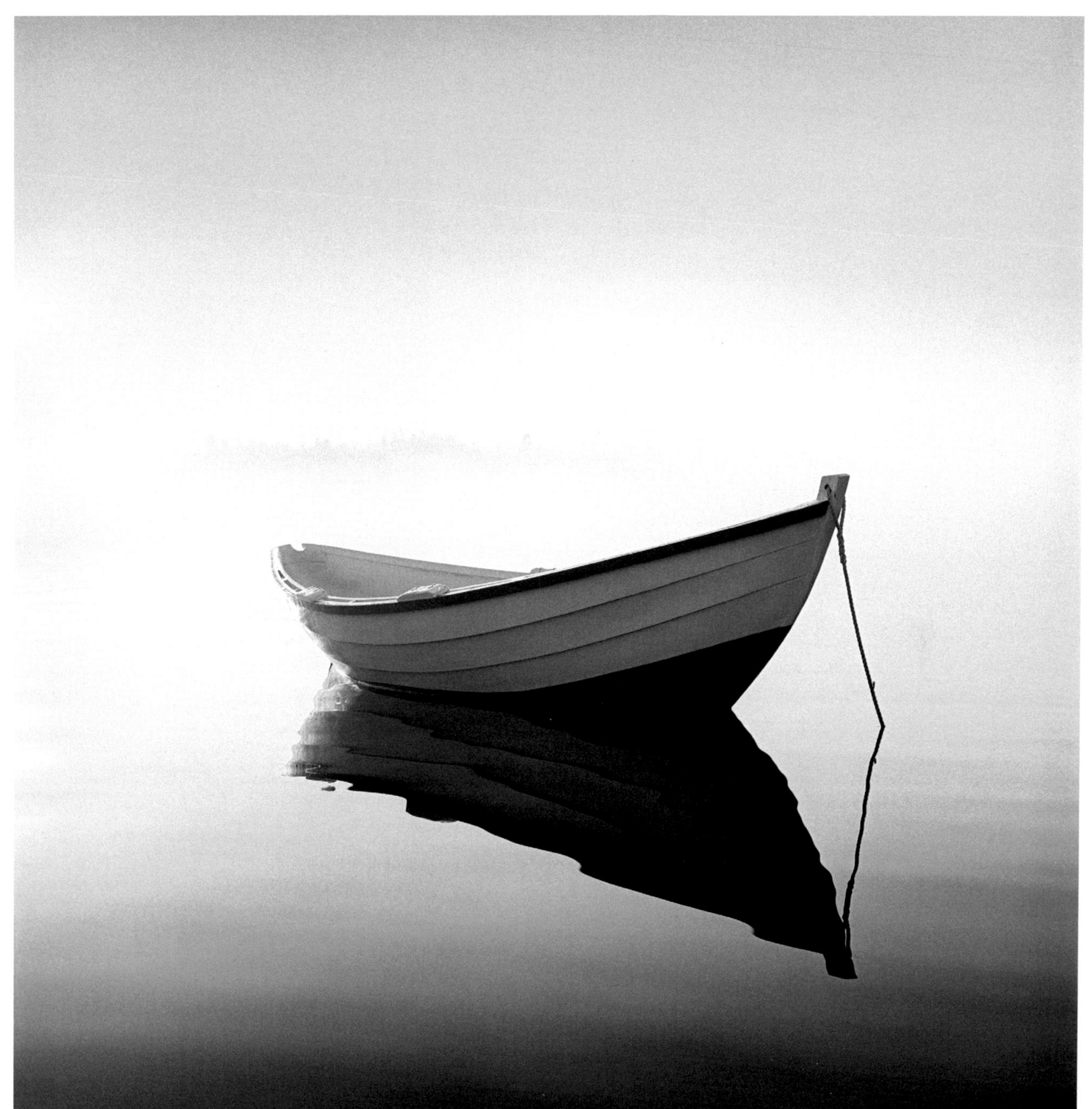

WoodenBoat School, Brooklin, Maine, 2010

The lesson that the sea teaches is that you must sail the wind you have. Not the one you wish you had, or the one you thought you would have, or the one you want to have. Accept reality. You have to live with what comes.

—NANCY GRIFFITH

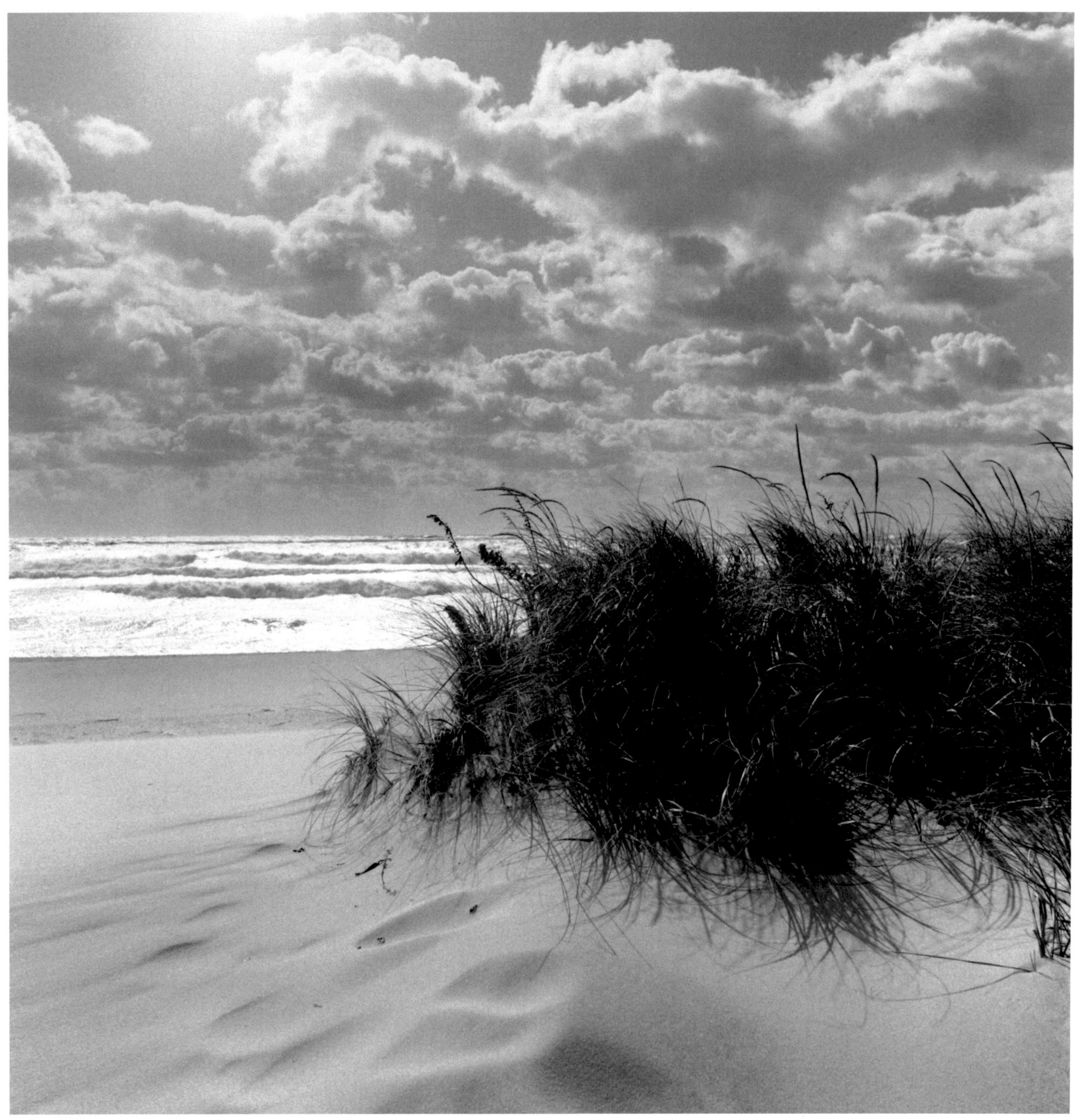

Martha's Vineyard, Massachusetts, 2006

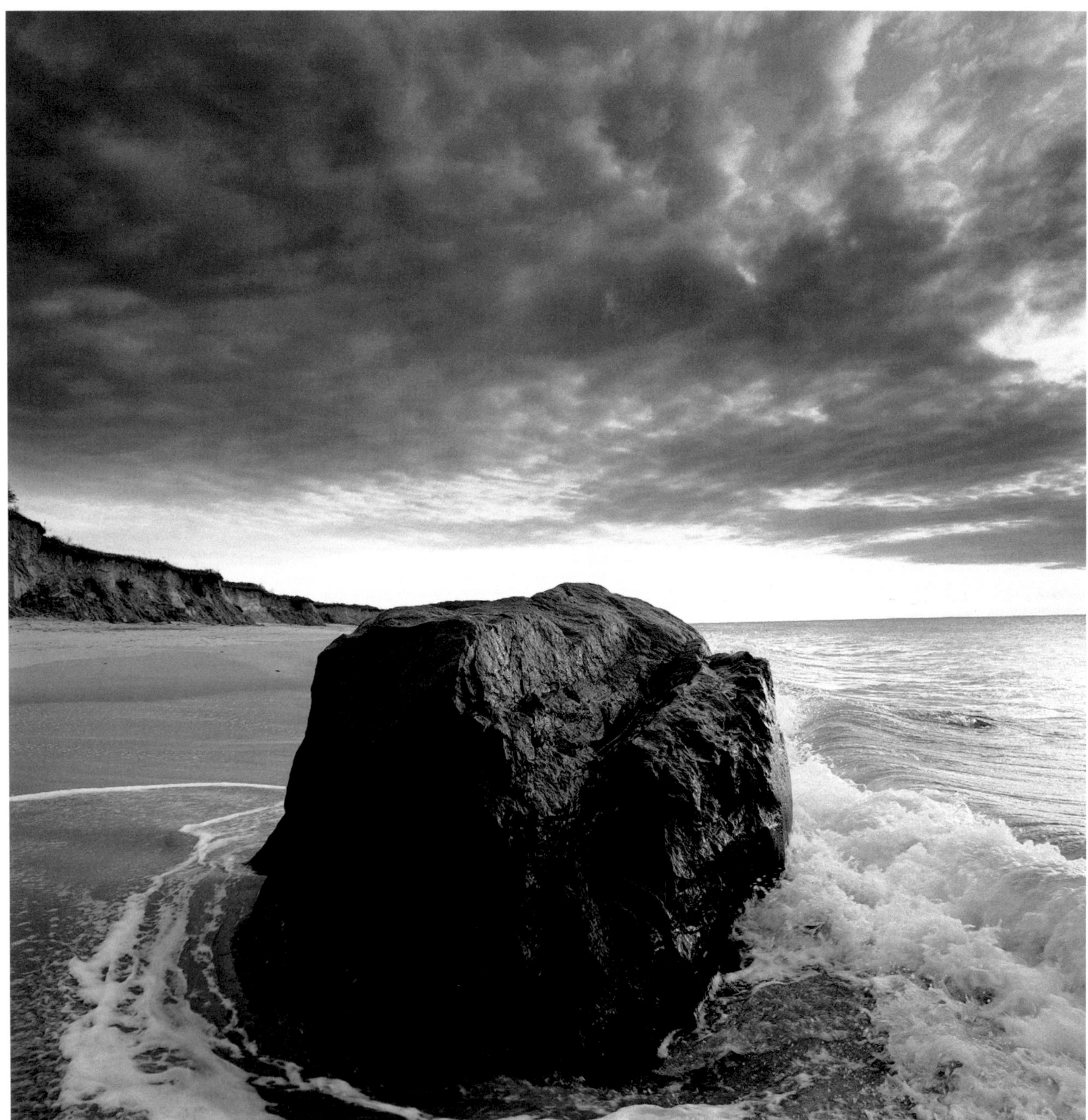

Martha's Vineyard, Massachusetts, 2006

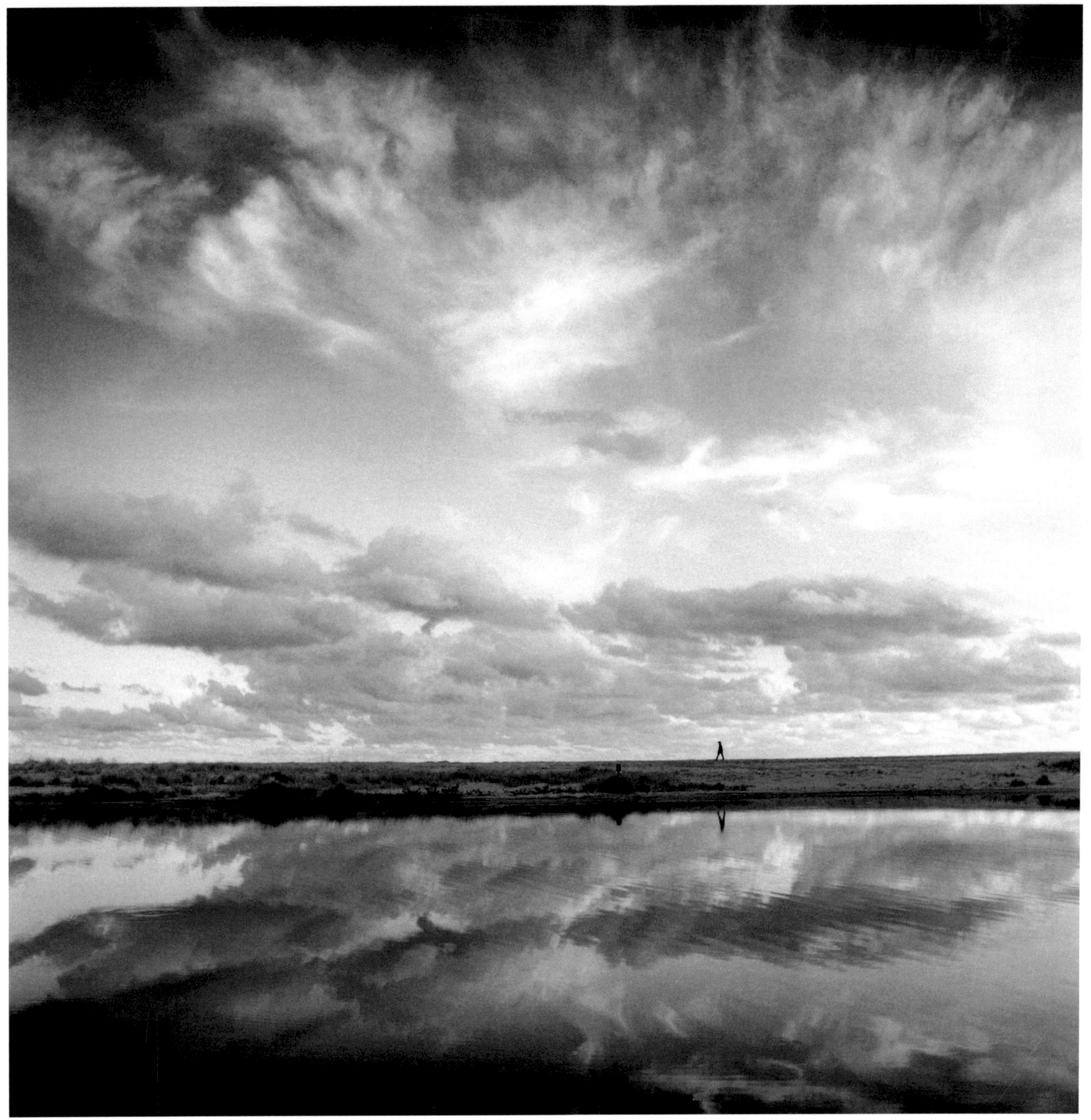

Martha's Vineyard, Massachusetts, 2003

*I believe silence is the
new luxury.*

———————————

—ERLING KAGGE

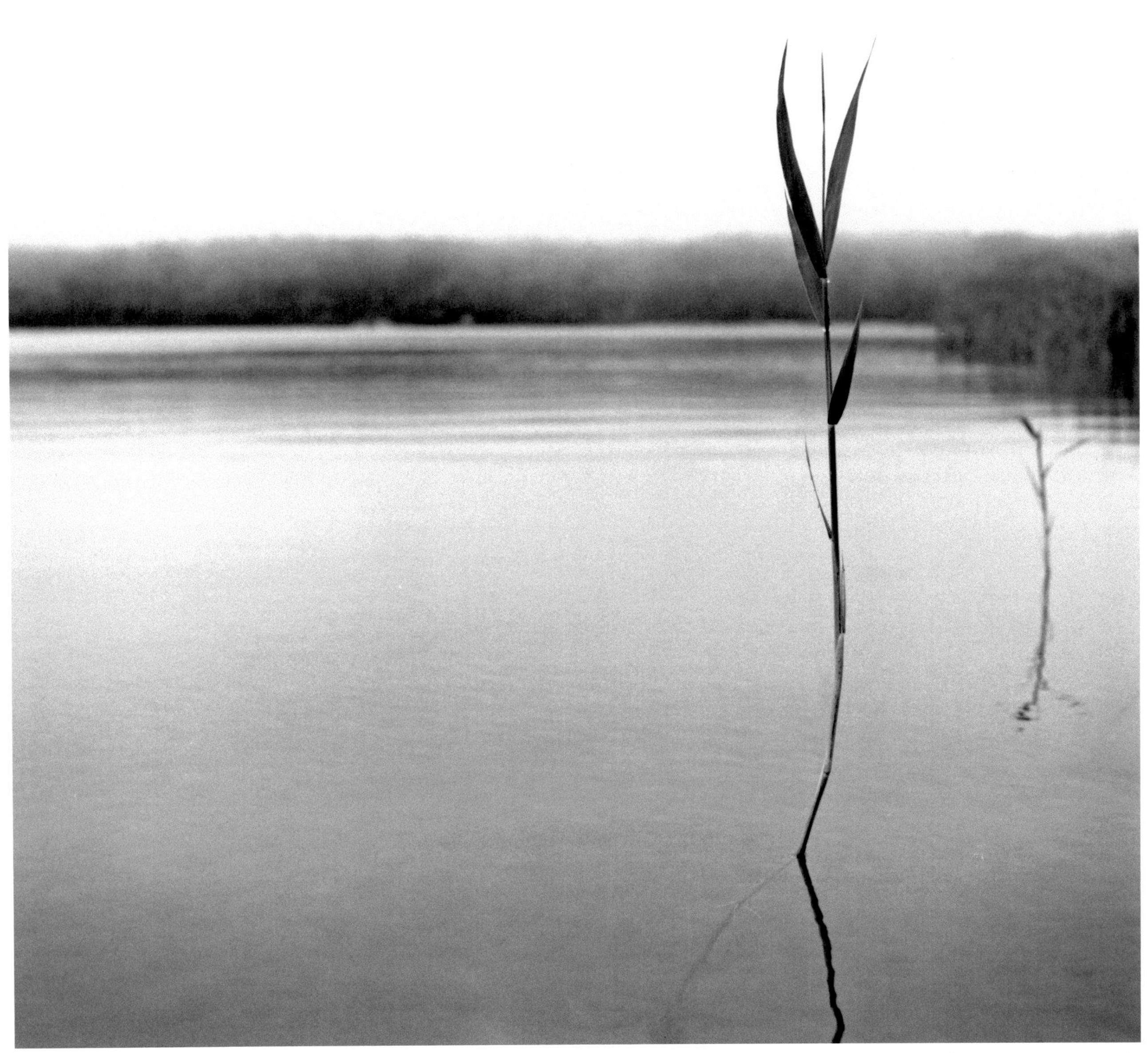

Nickerson State Park, Cape Cod, Massachusetts, 2015

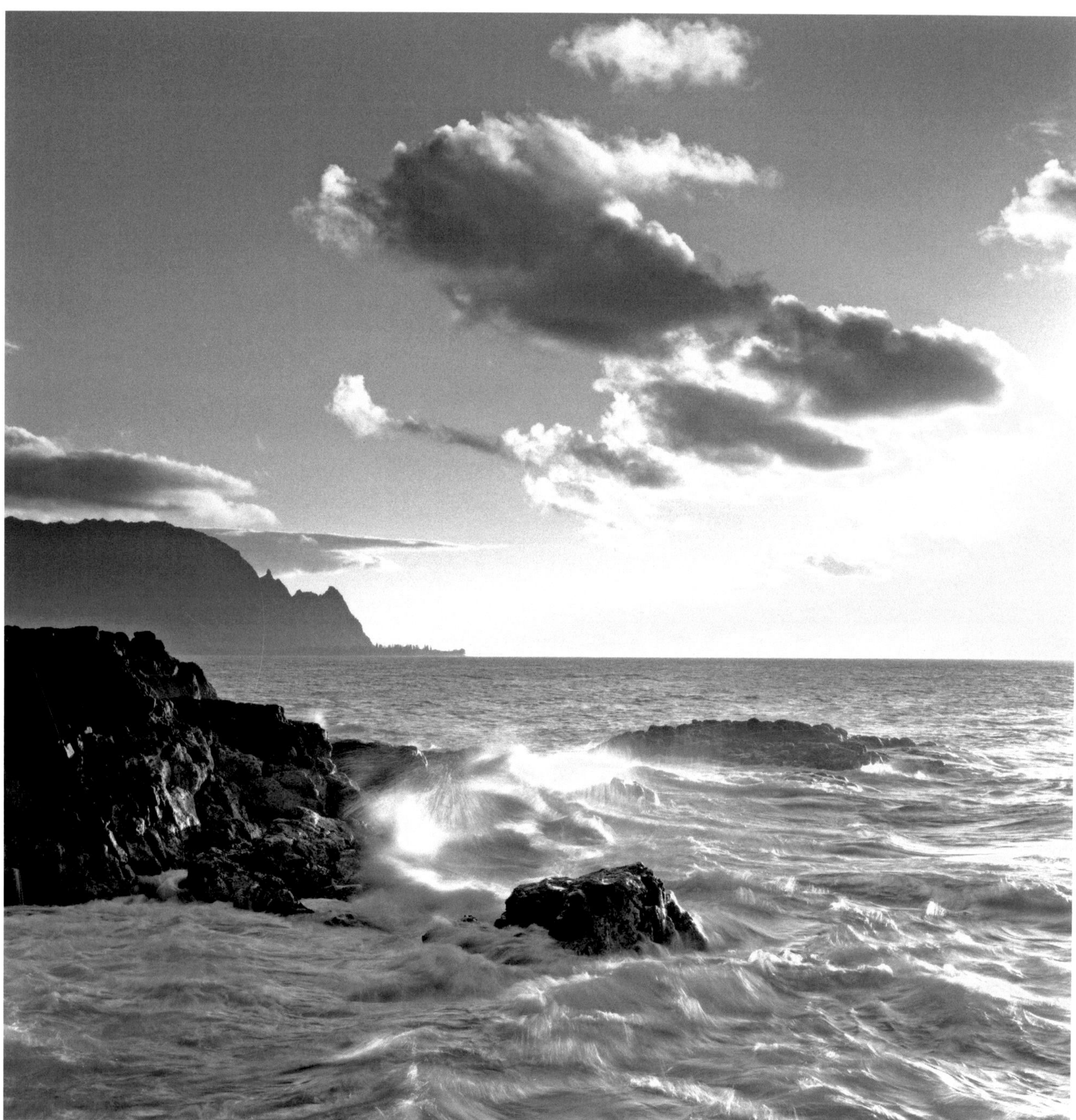

Queen's Bath, Kauai, Hawaii, 2014

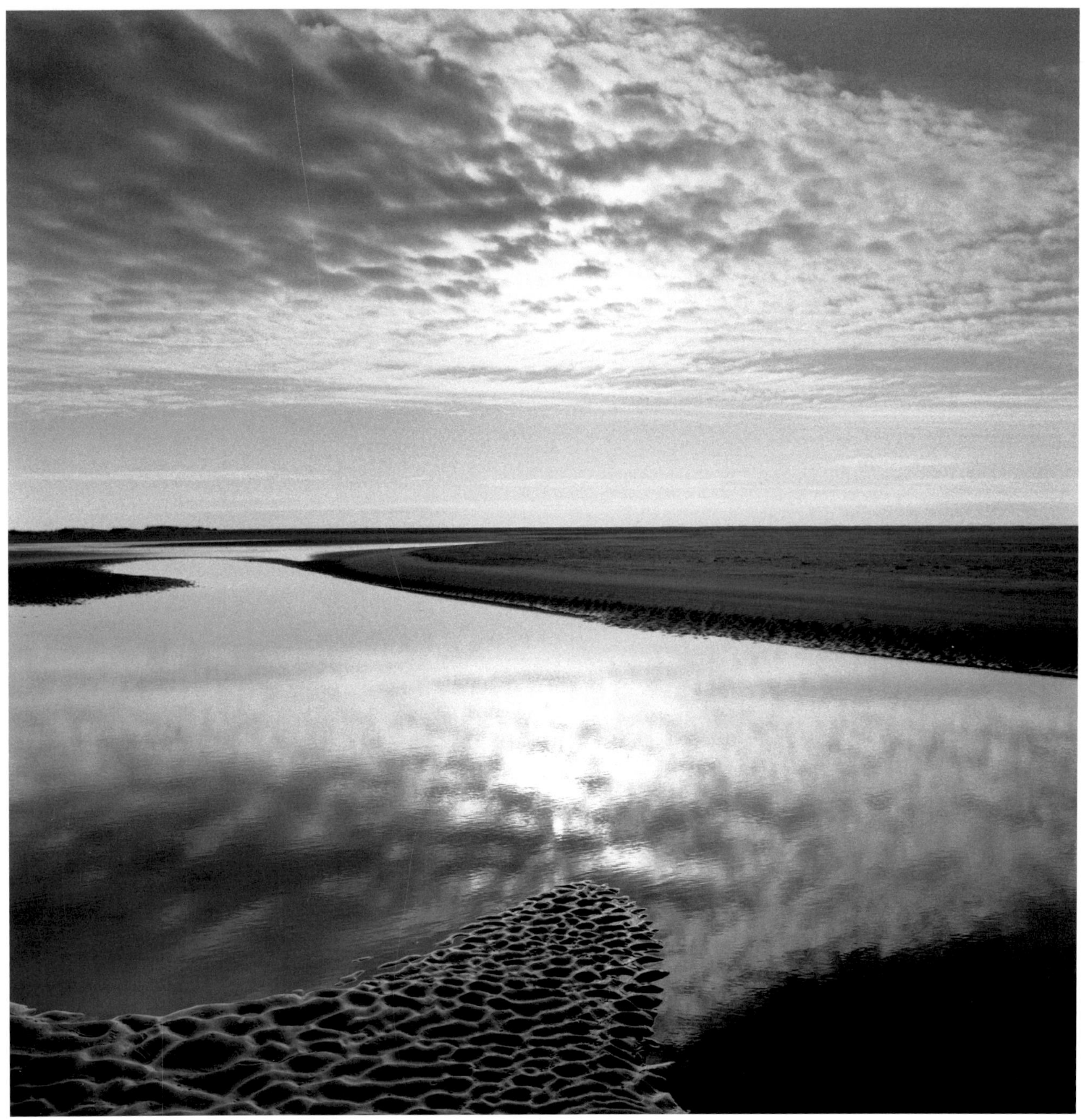

Popham Beach State Park, Maine, 2007

Wash yourself of yourself.

———————————————

—RUMI

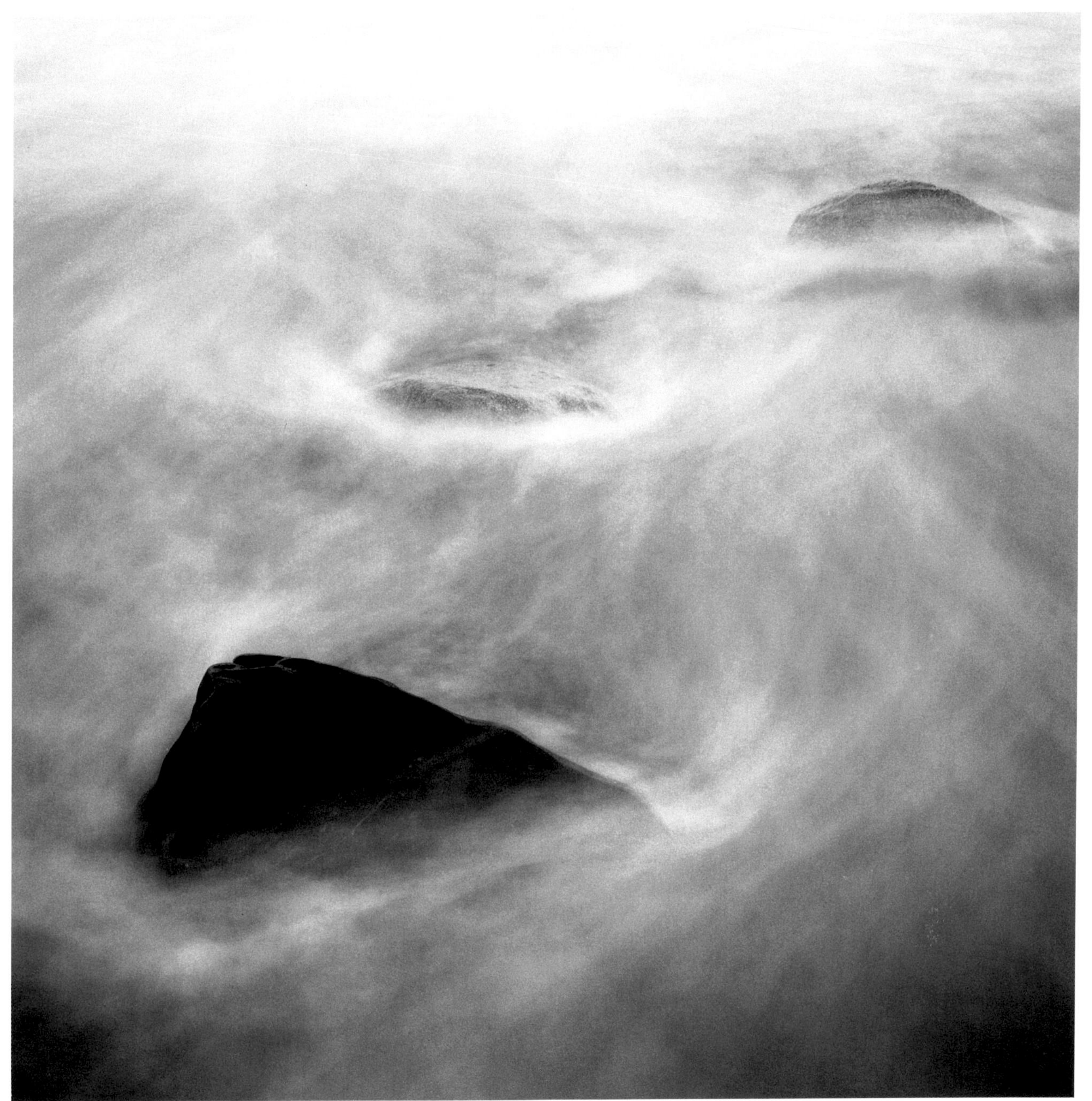

Martha's Vineyard, Massachusetts, 1999

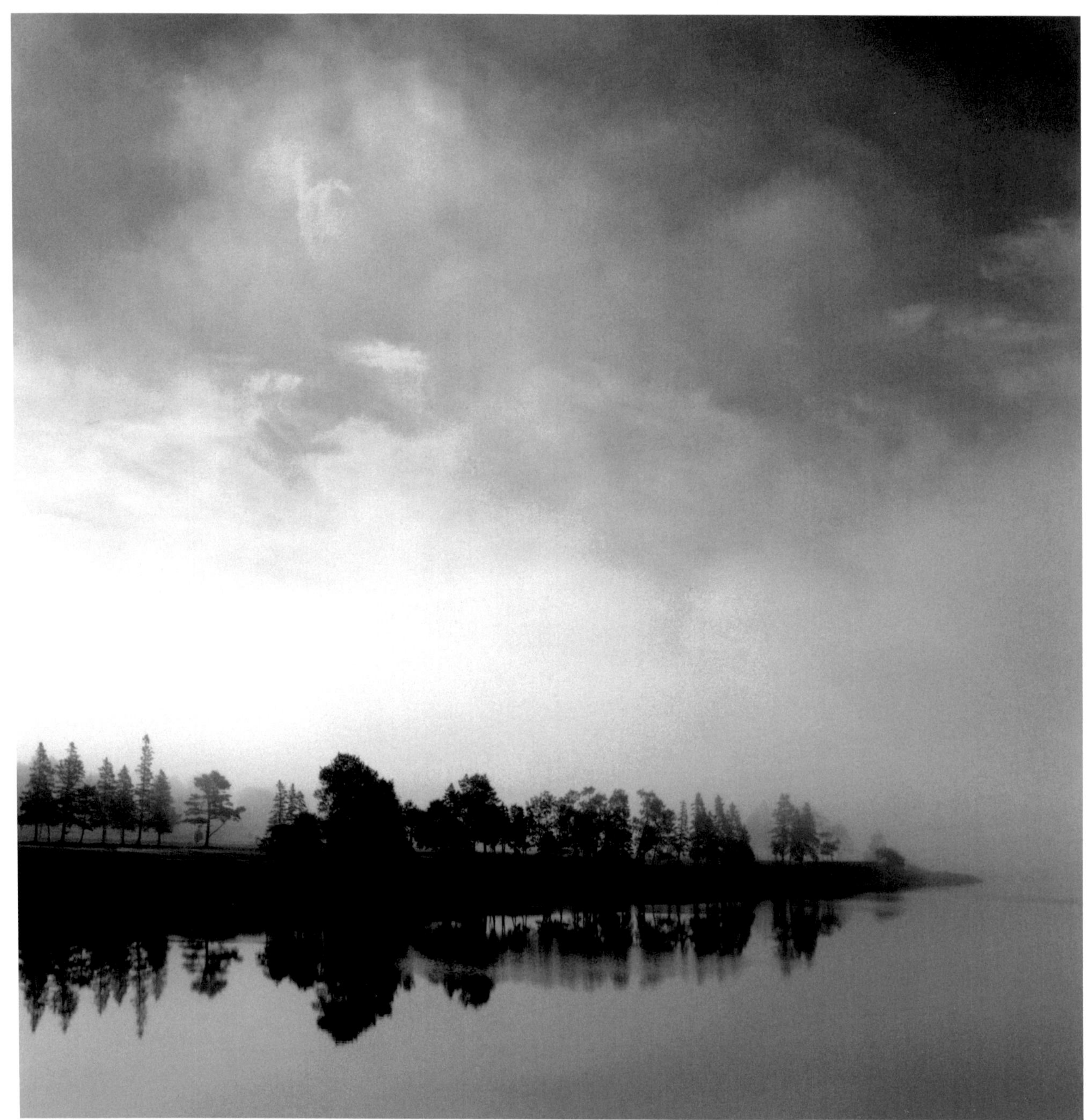

Acadia National Park, Mount Desert Island, Maine, 2011

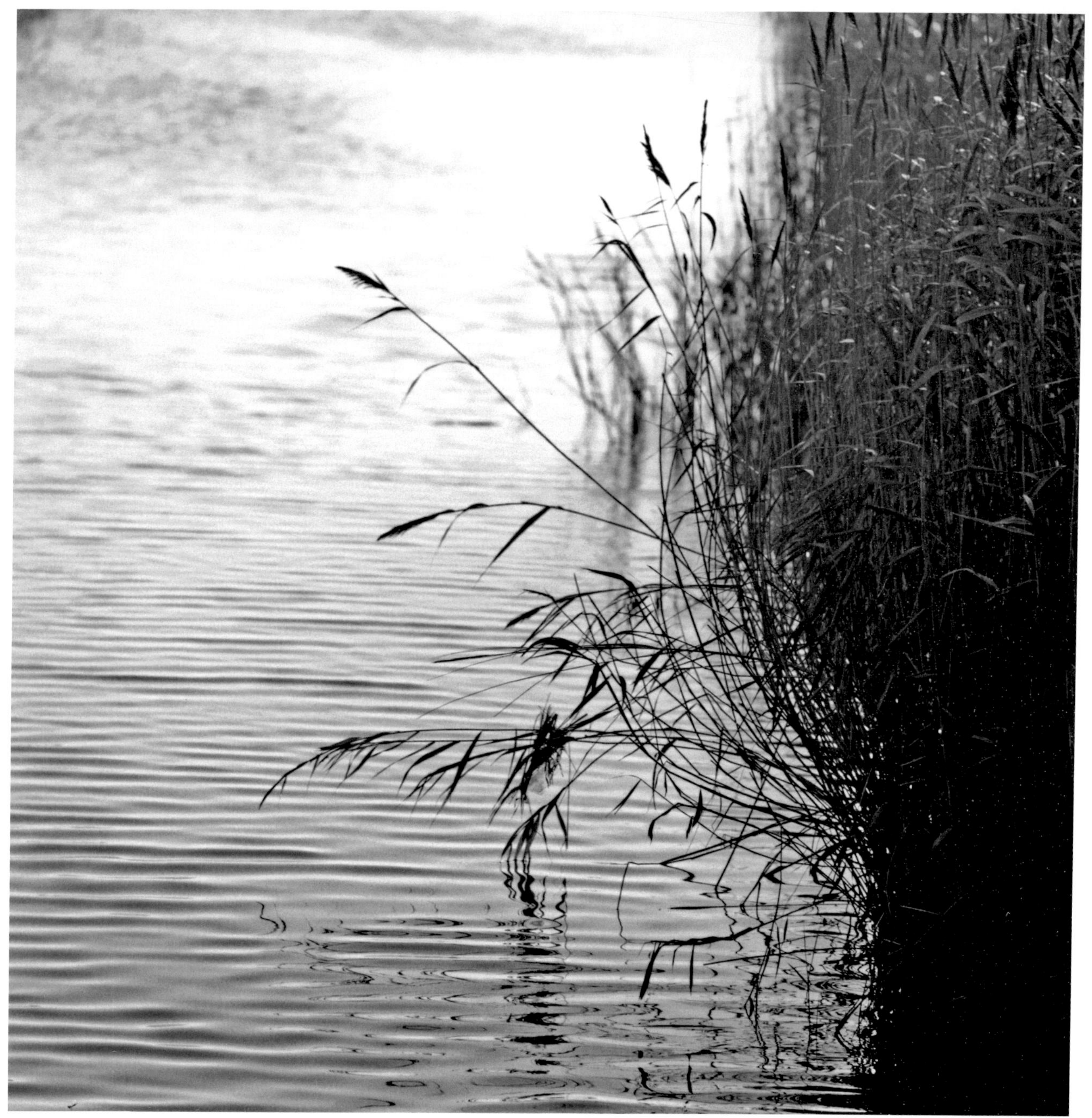

Martha's Vineyard, Massachusetts, 2011

*Nothing is softer or more
flexible than water,
yet nothing can resist it.*

———————————

—LAO TZU

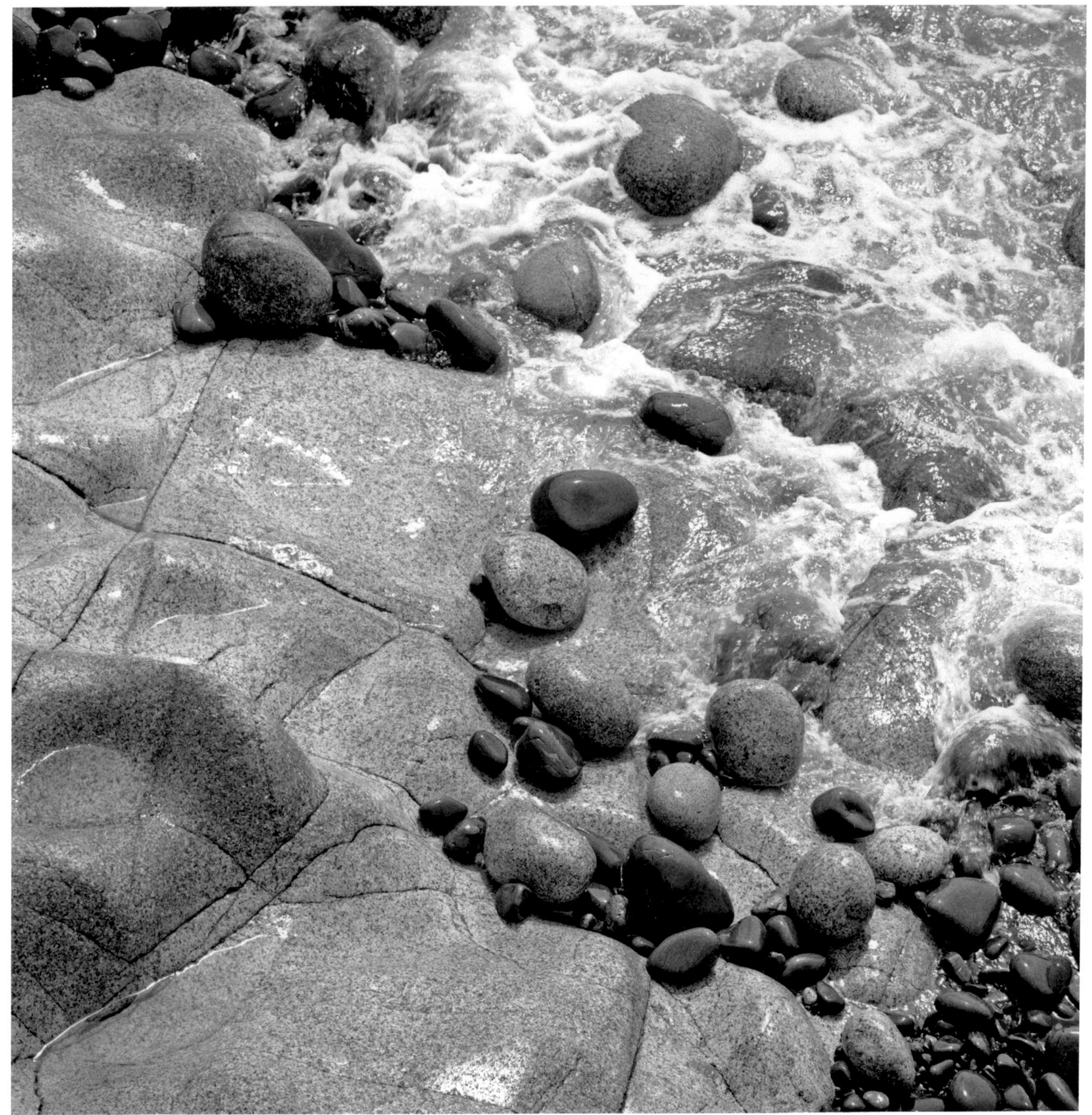

Penwith Heritage Coast, England, 2001

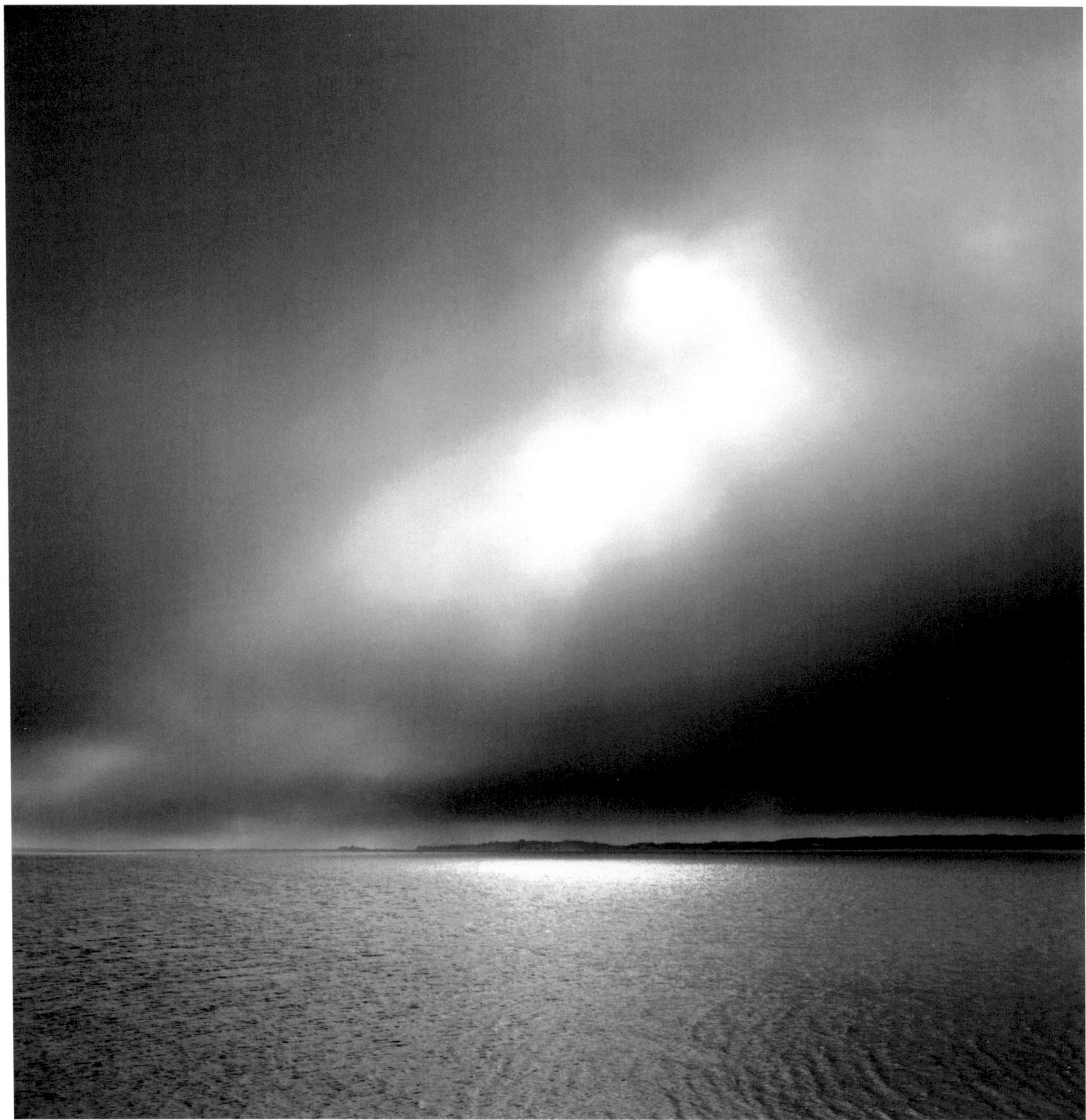

Martha's Vineyard, Massachusetts, 2001

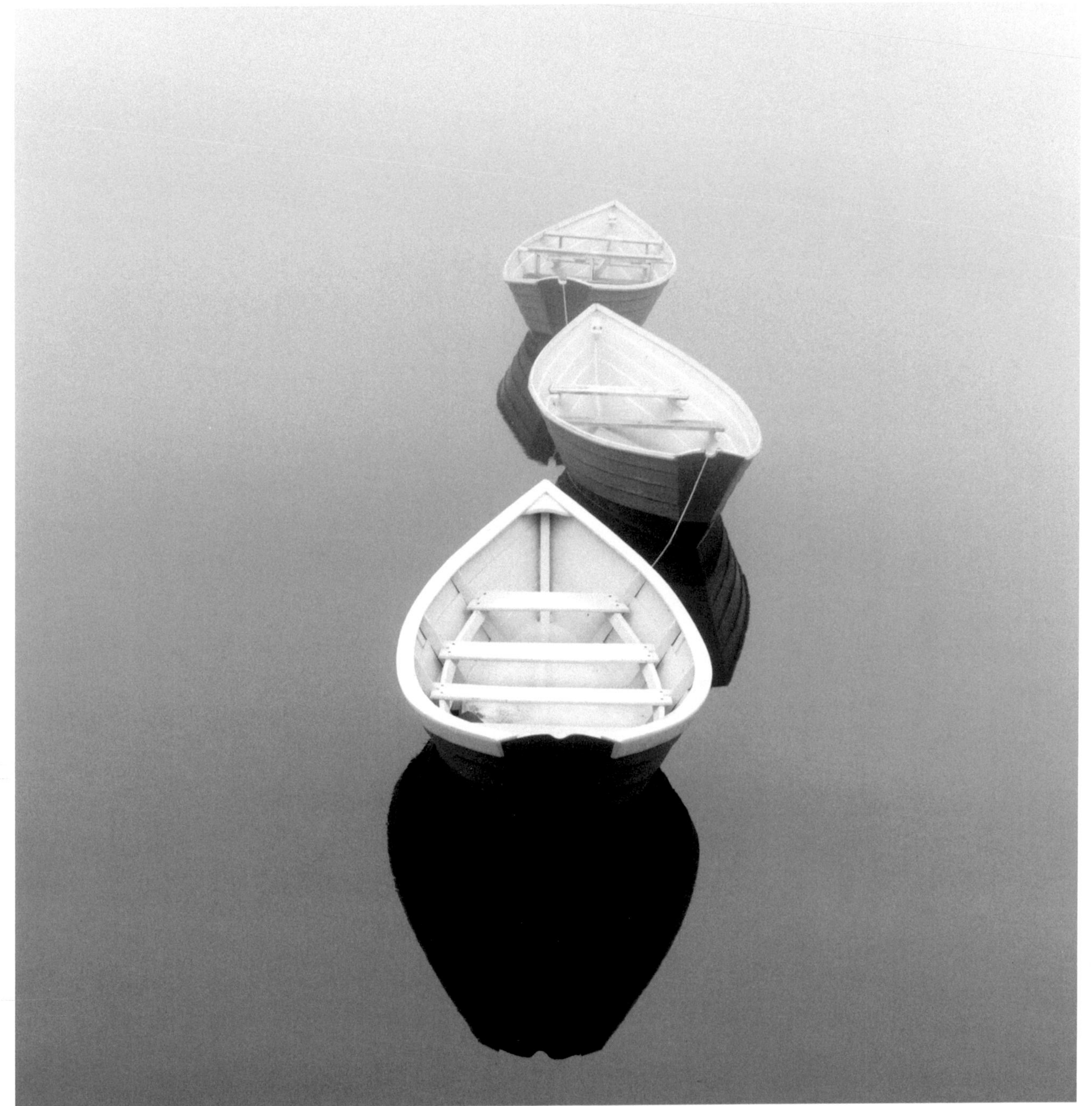

Kennebunkport, Maine, 2011

*At sea a fellow comes out.
Salt water is like wine in
that respect.*

———————————

—HERMAN MELVILLE

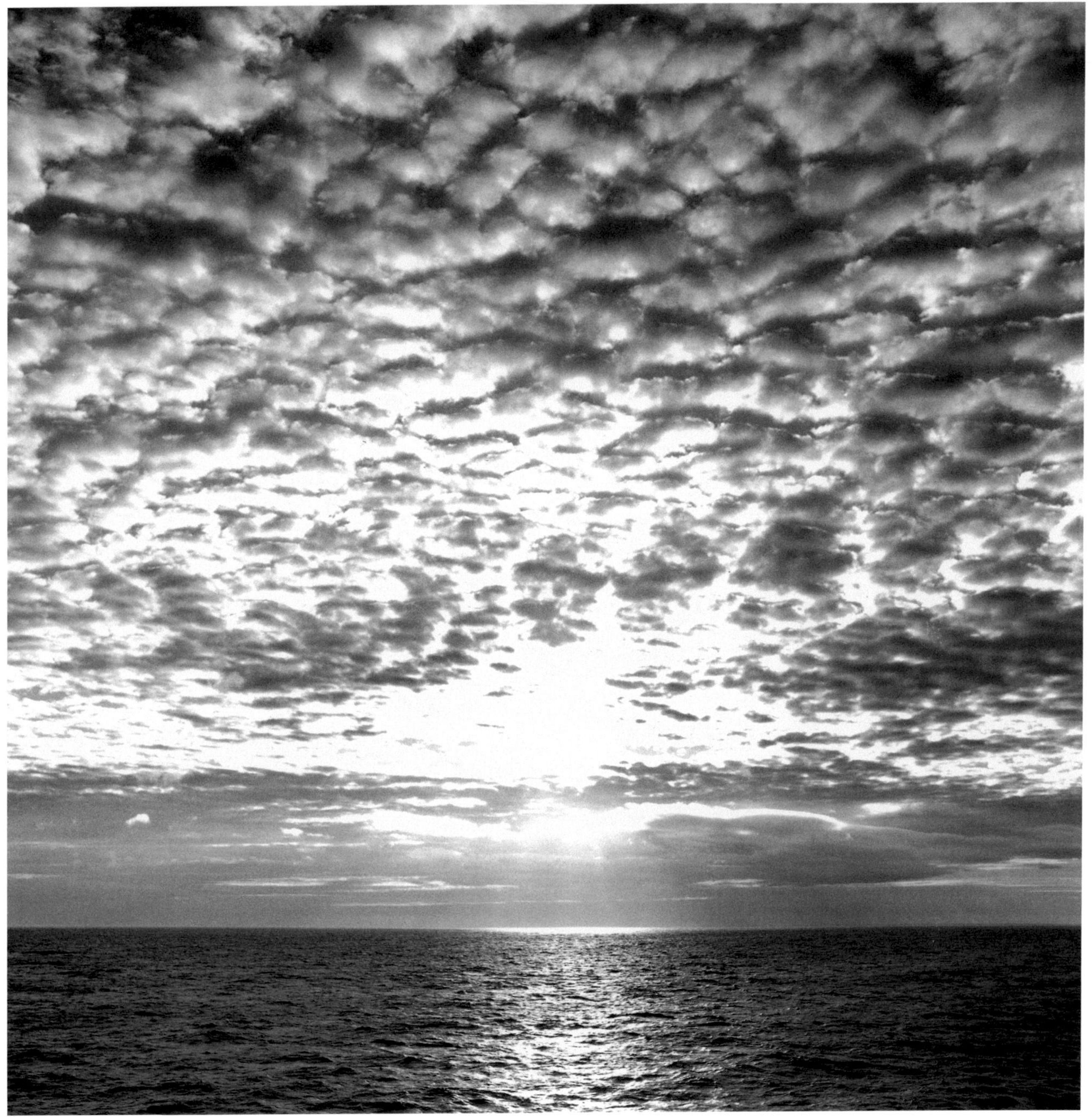

Nantucket, Massachusetts, 2005

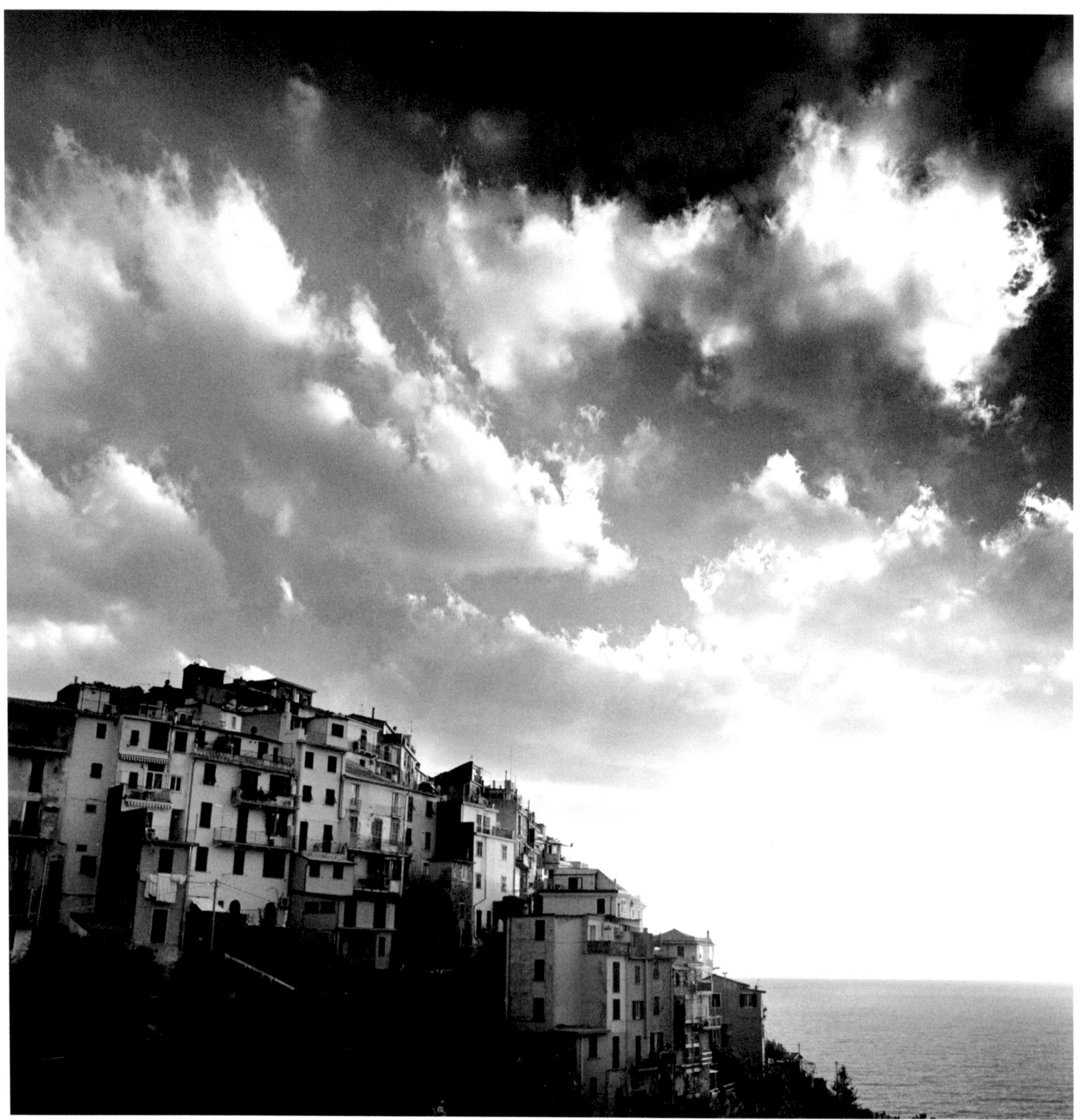

Manarola, Cinque Tierra, Italy, 2013

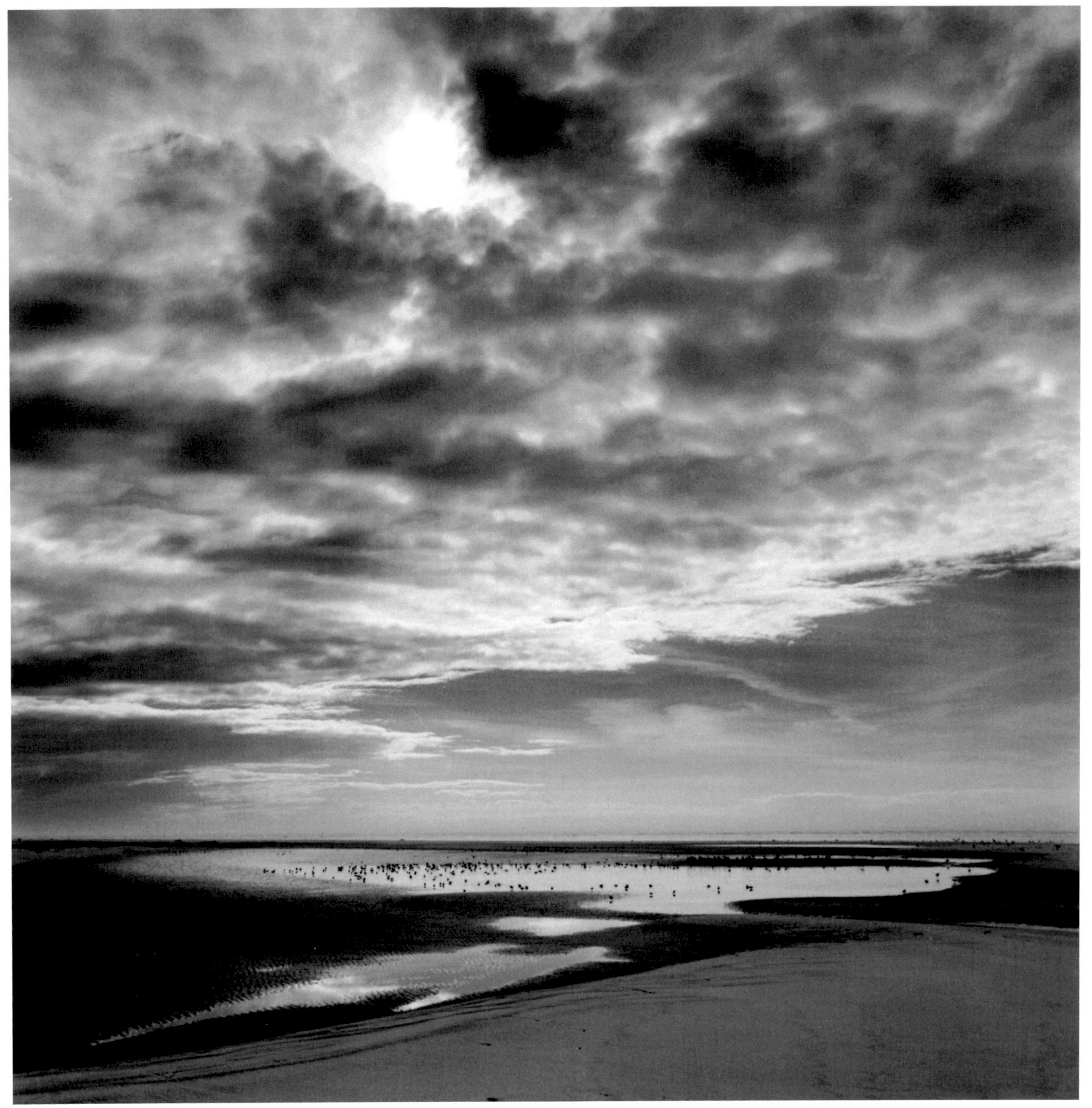

Topsail Beach, North Carolina, 2017

*The cure for anything is salt water—
sweat, tears, or the sea.*

—ISAK DINESEN

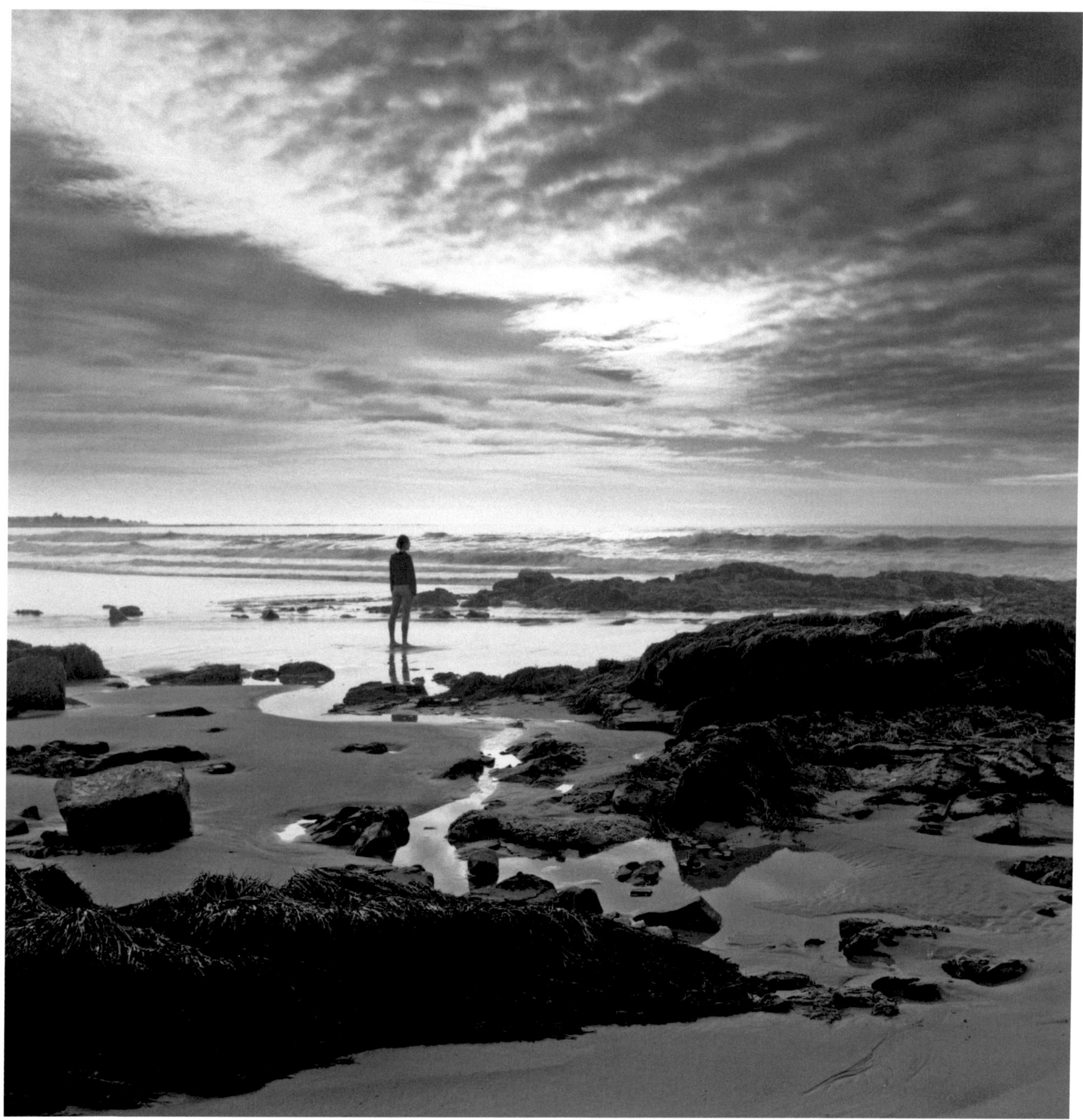

York Beach, Maine, 2012

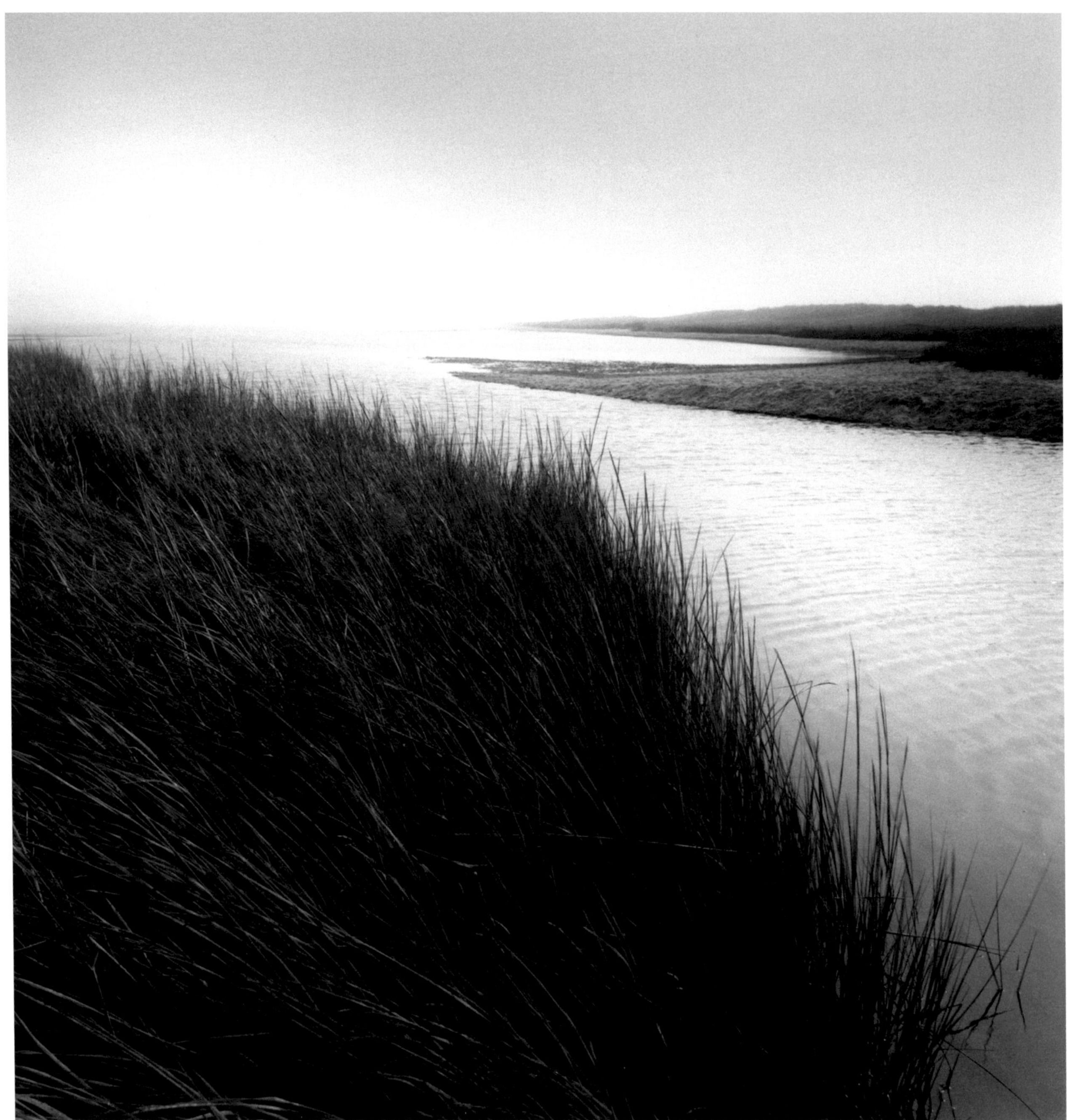

Martha's Vineyard, Massachusetts, 2011

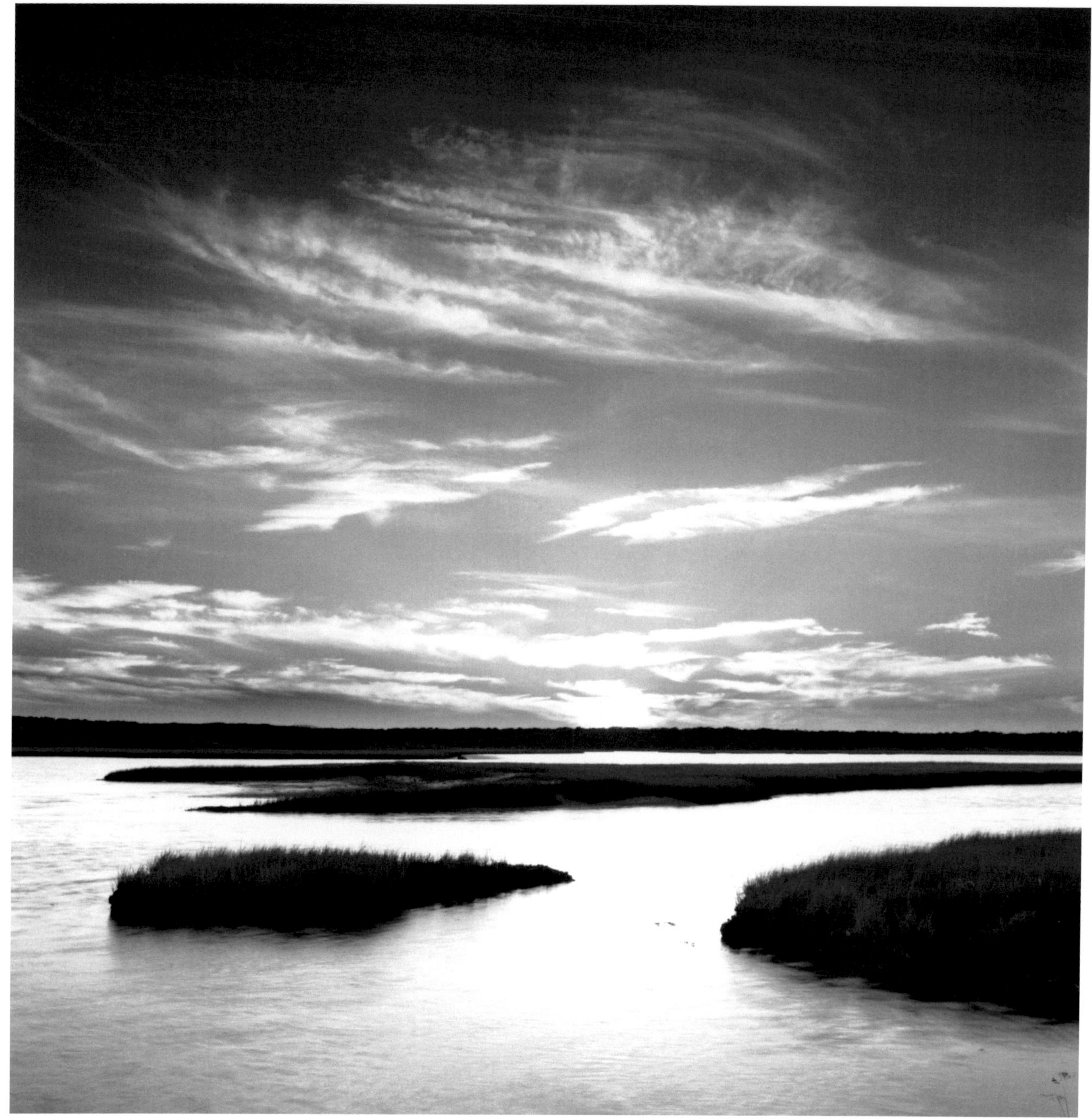

Martha's Vineyard, Massachusetts, 2001

*To what
shall I compare the world?
It is like the wake
vanishing behind a boat
that has rowed away at dawn.*

—SAMI MANZEI

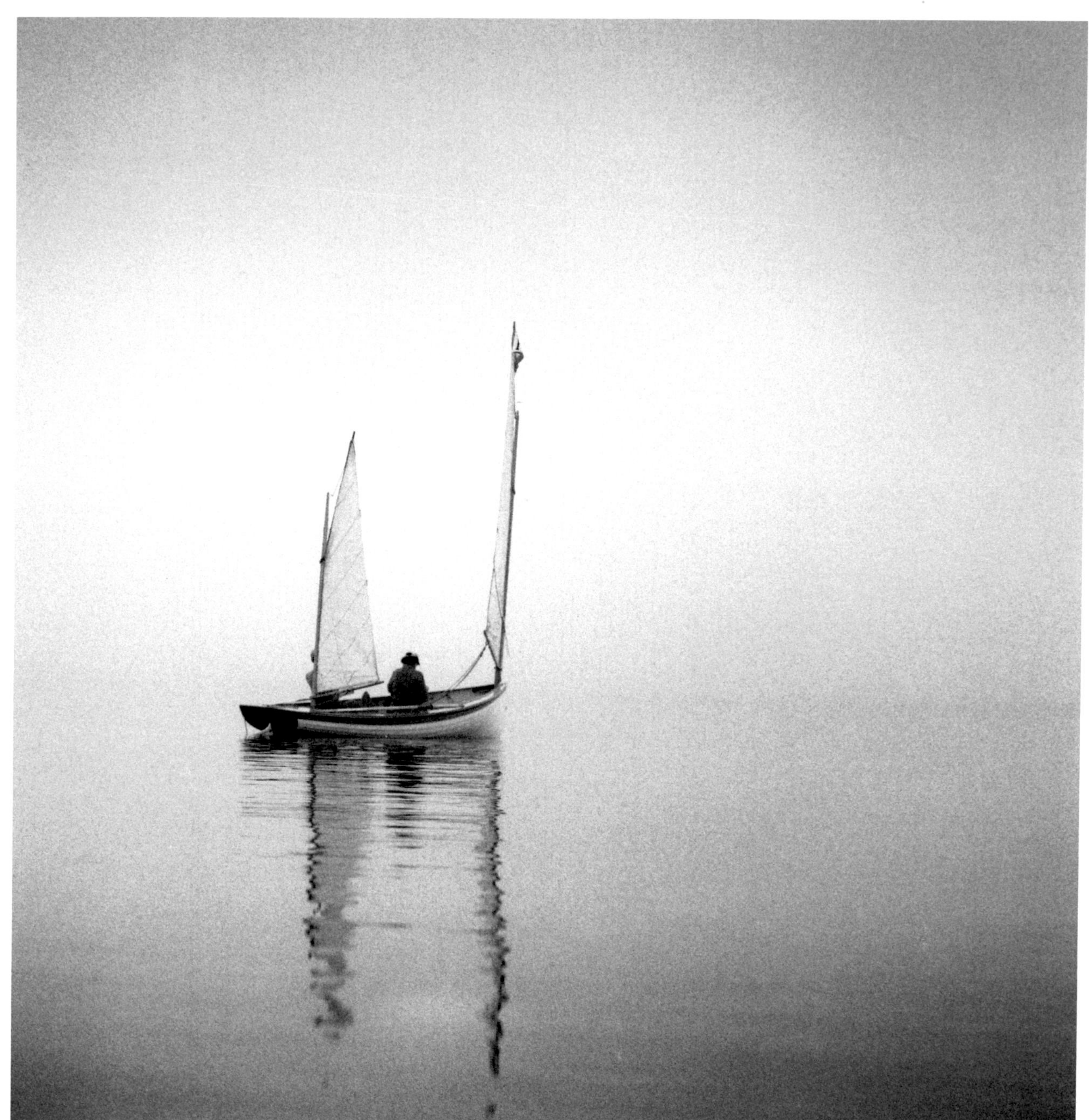

WoodenBoat School, Brooklin, Maine, 2008

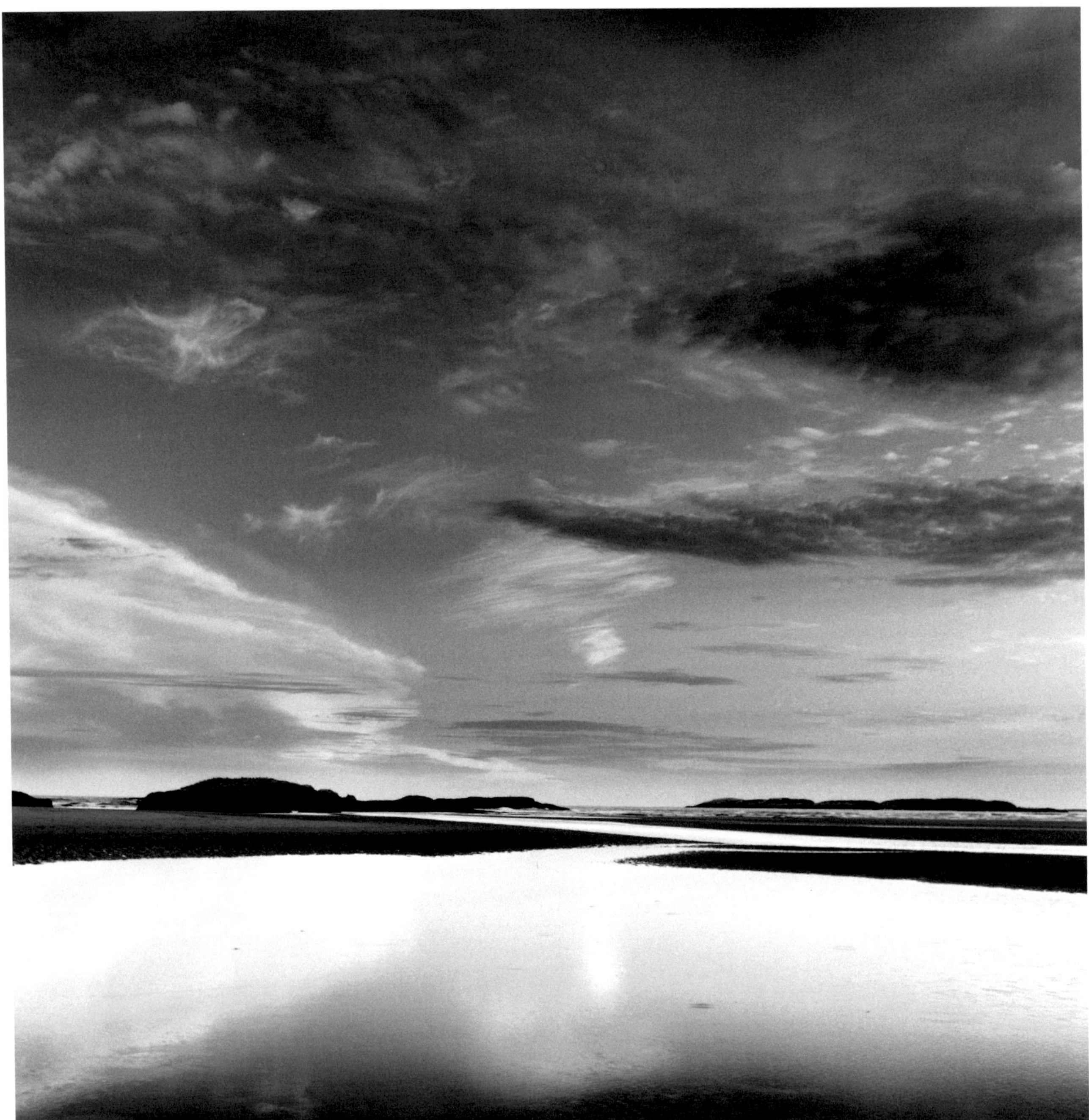

Popham Beach State Park, Maine, 2002

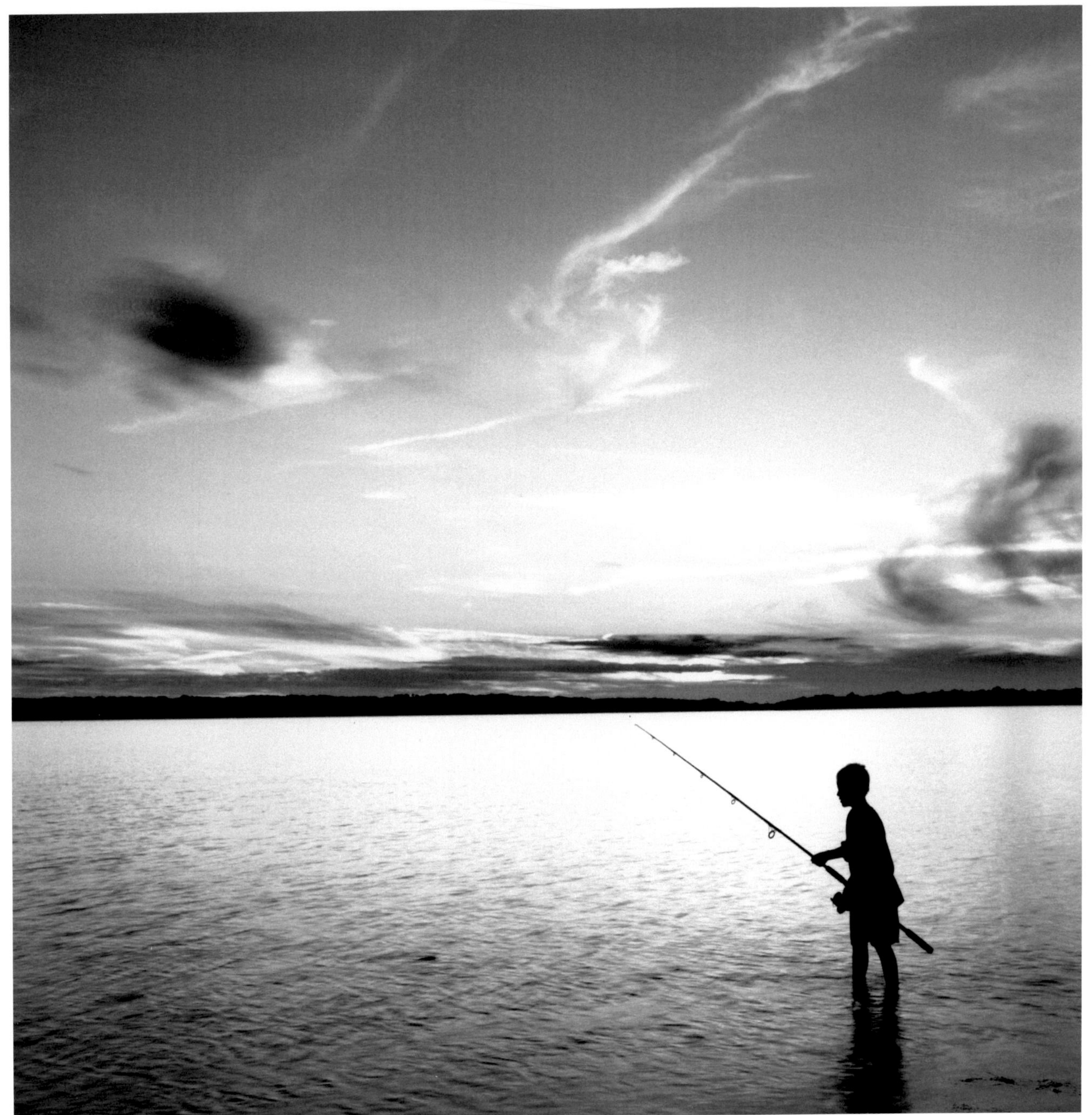

Martha's Vineyard, Massachusetts, 2001

*Imperfection is a form
of freedom.*

—————————————

—ANH NGO

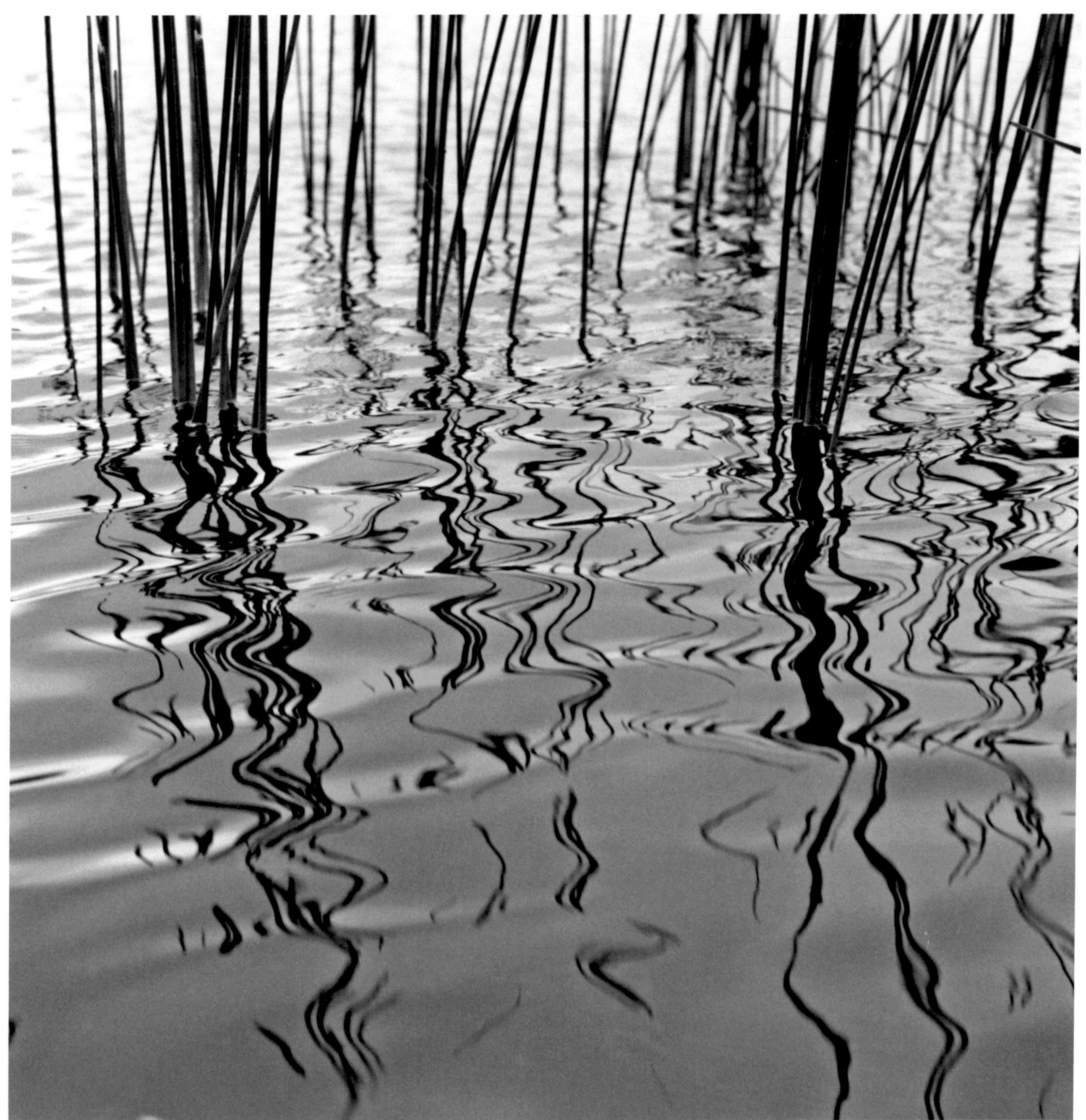

Nickerson State Park, Cape Cod, Massachusetts, 2015

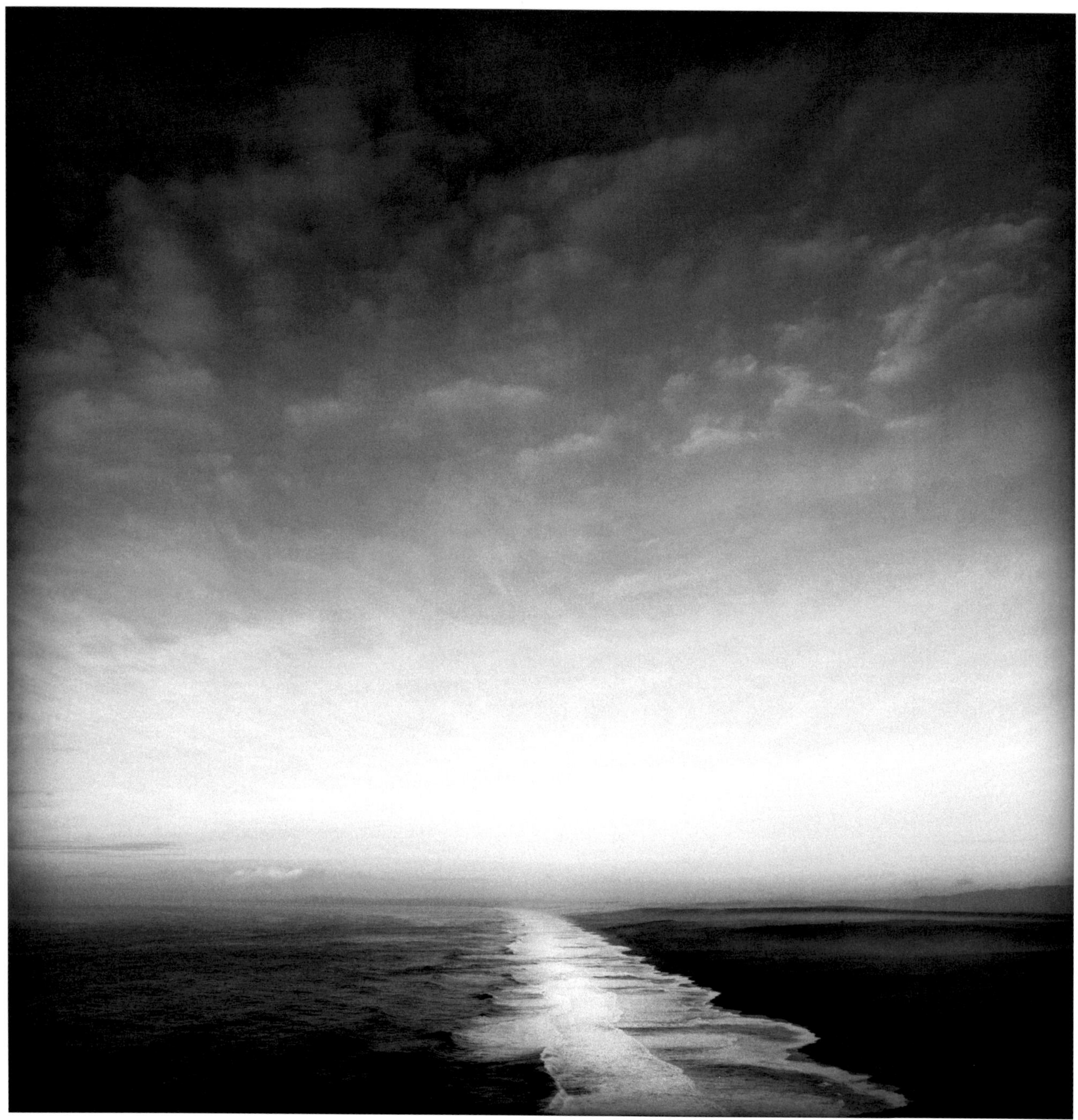

Point Reyes, California, 1999

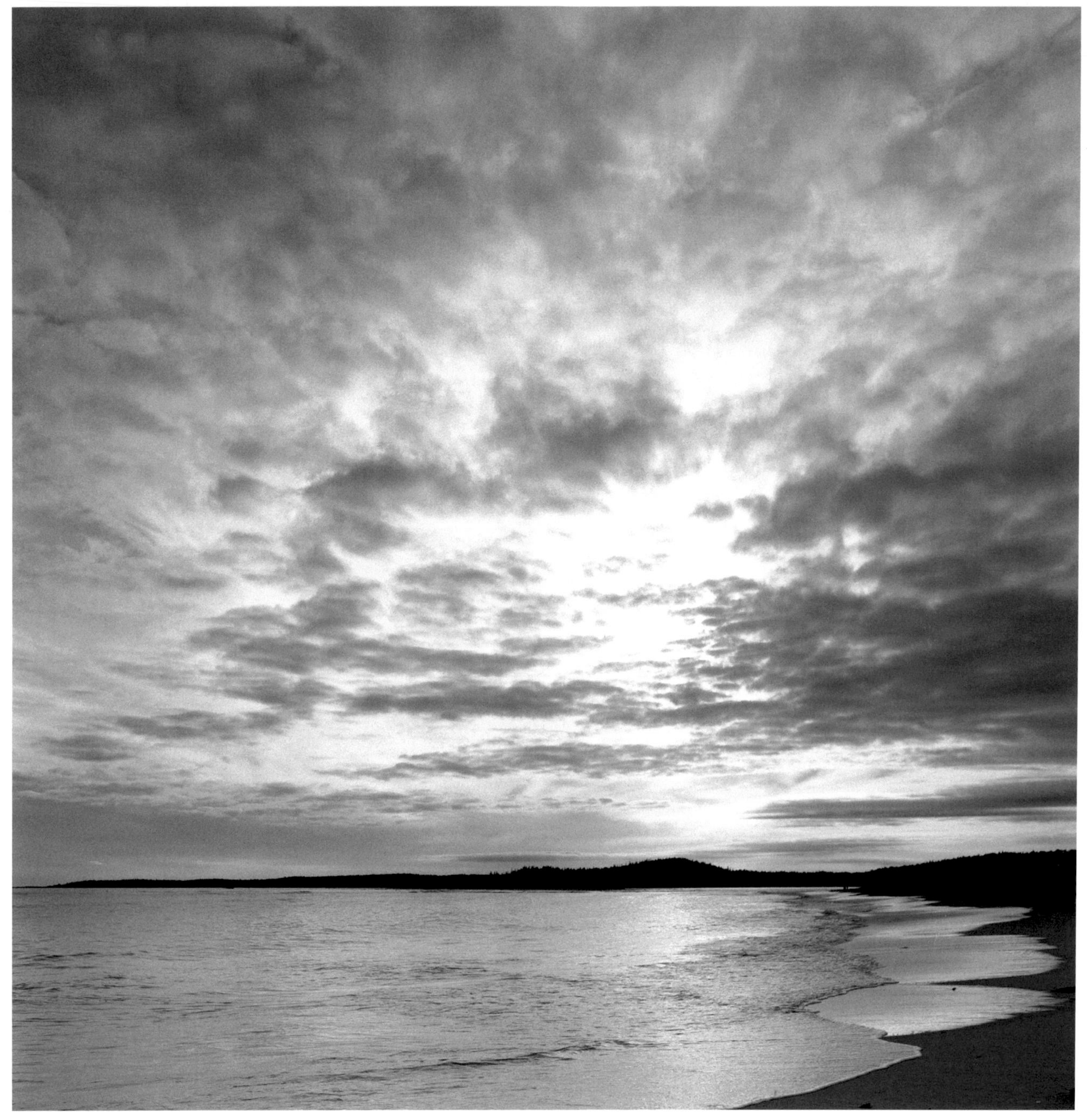

Martha's Vineyard, Massachusetts, 2006

*The real voyage of discovery
consists not in seeing
new landscapes, but in
having new eyes.*

—MARCEL PROUST

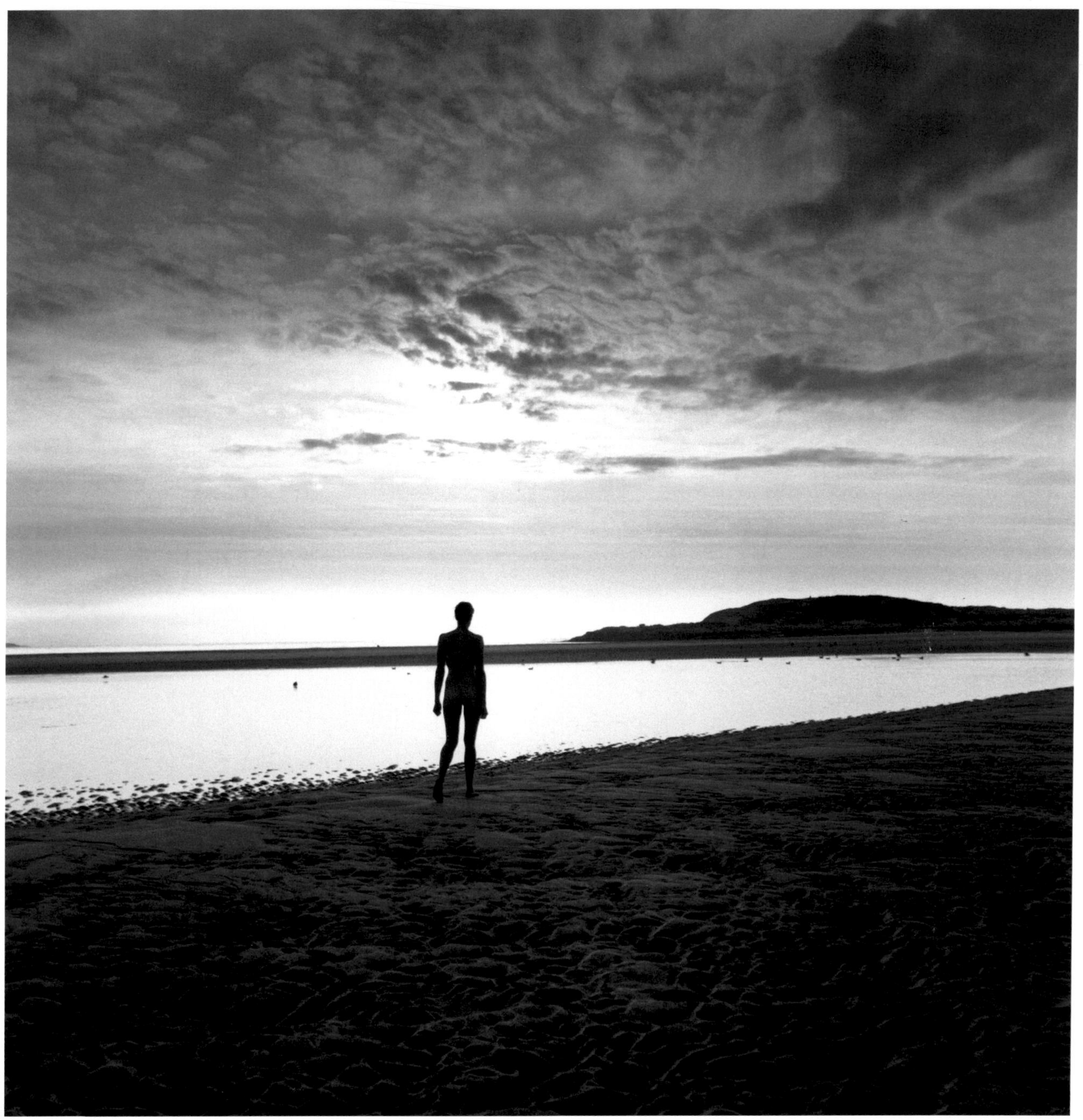

Popham Beach State Park, Maine, 2012

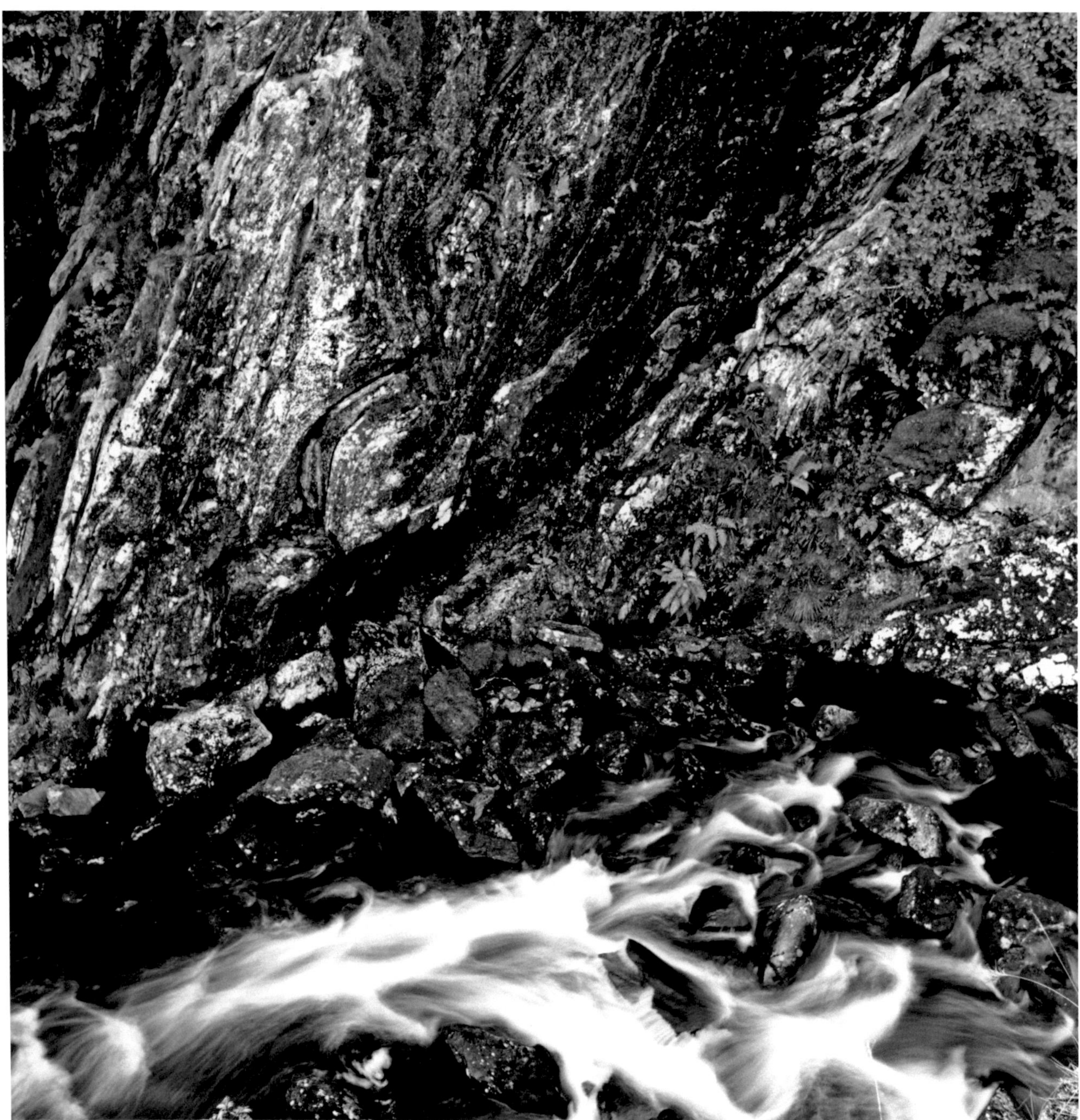

Penwith Heritage Coast, England, 2001

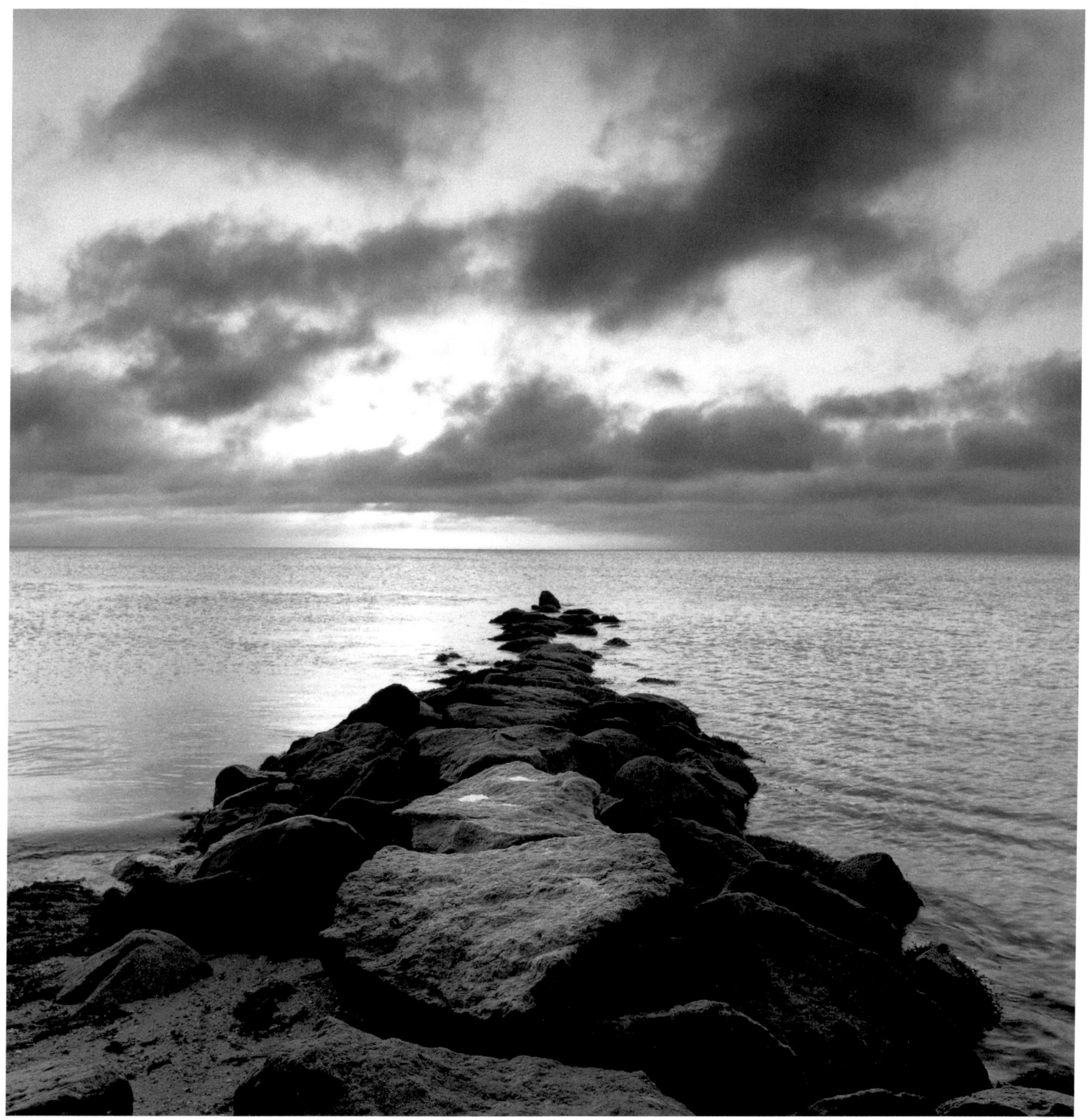

Martha's Vineyard, Massachusetts, 2001

If the ocean can calm itself, so can you. We are both salt water mixed with air.

—NAYYIRAH WAHEED

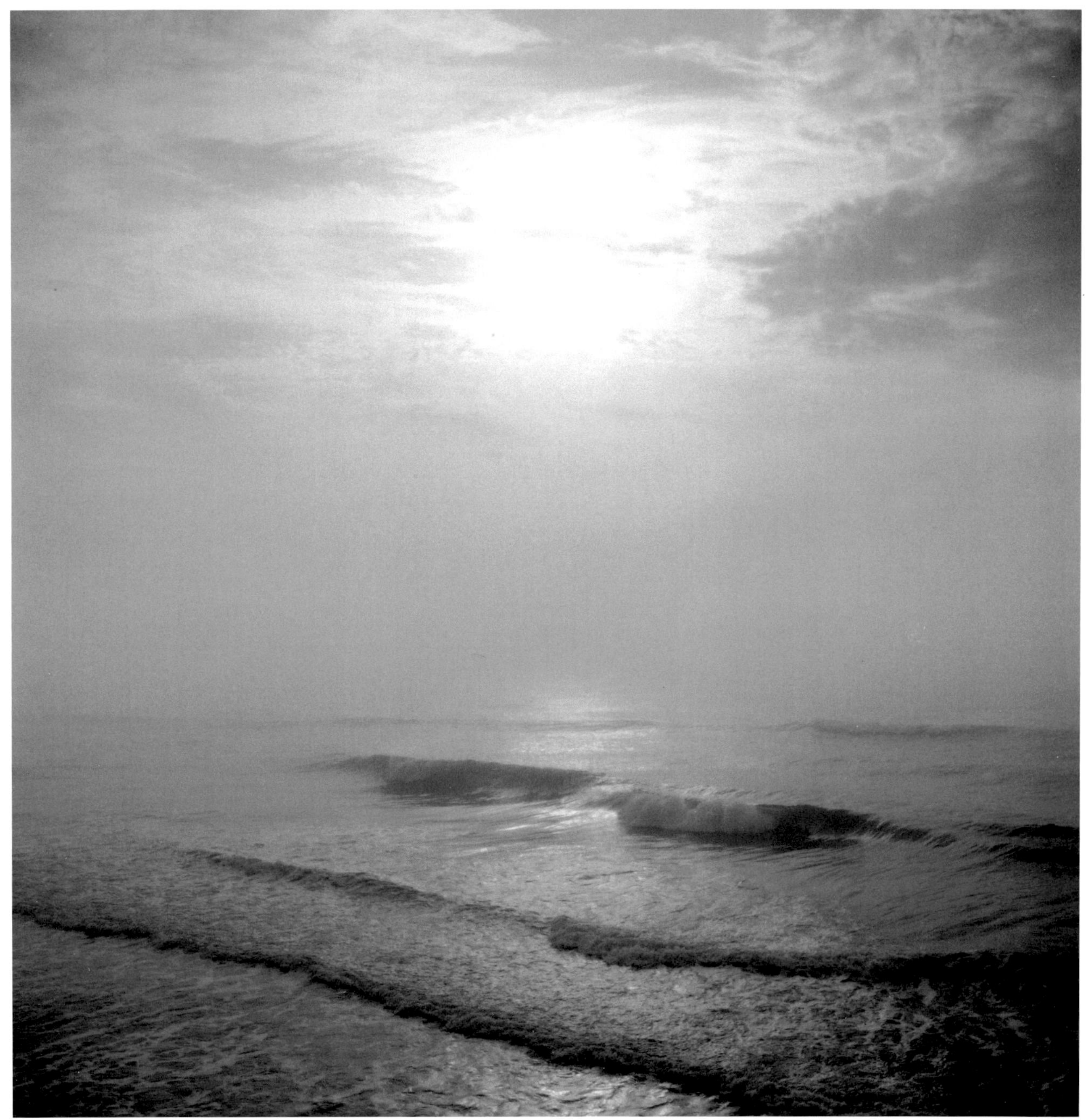

Topsail Beach, North Carolina, 2005

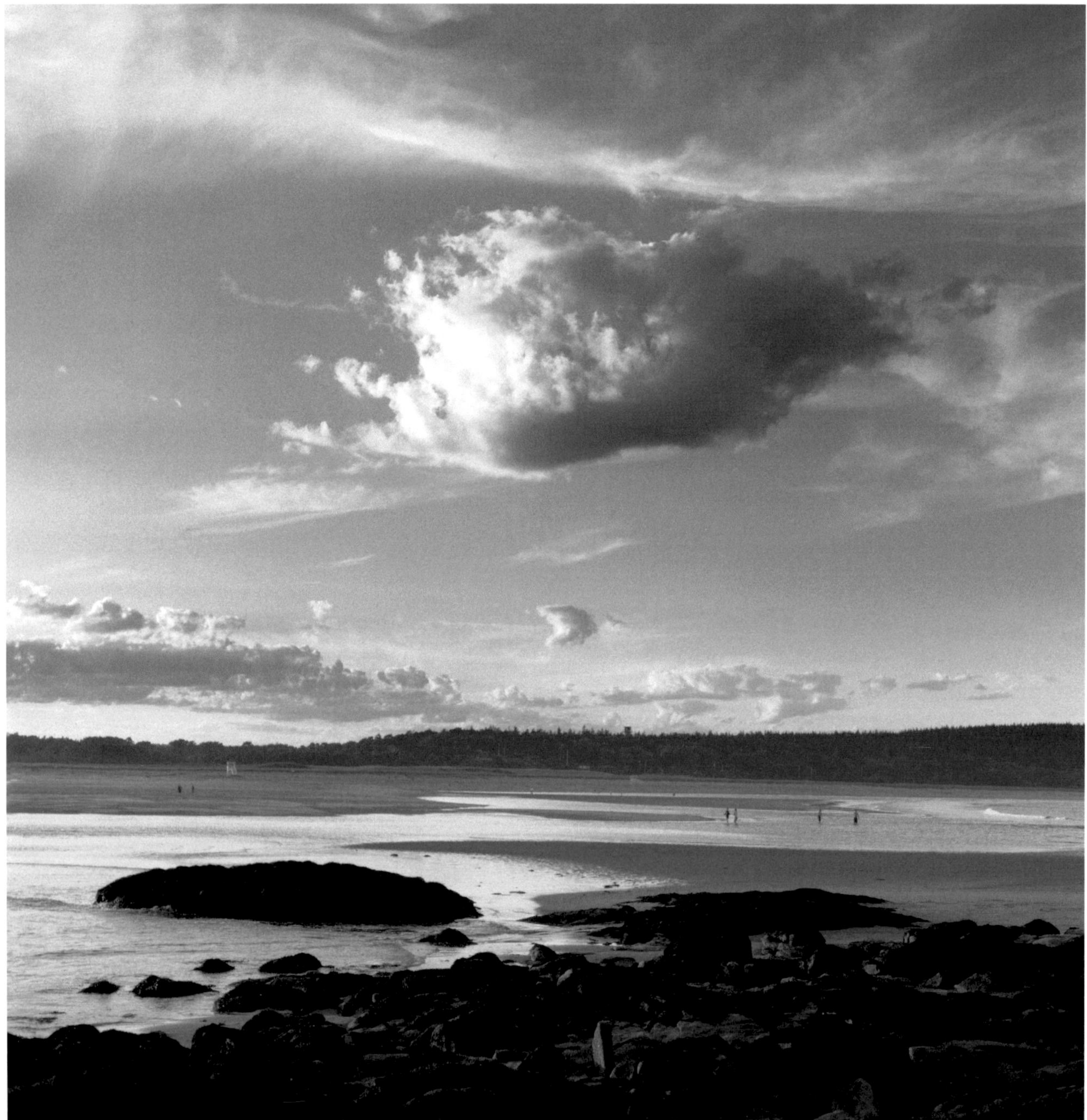

Popham Beach State Park, Maine, 2006

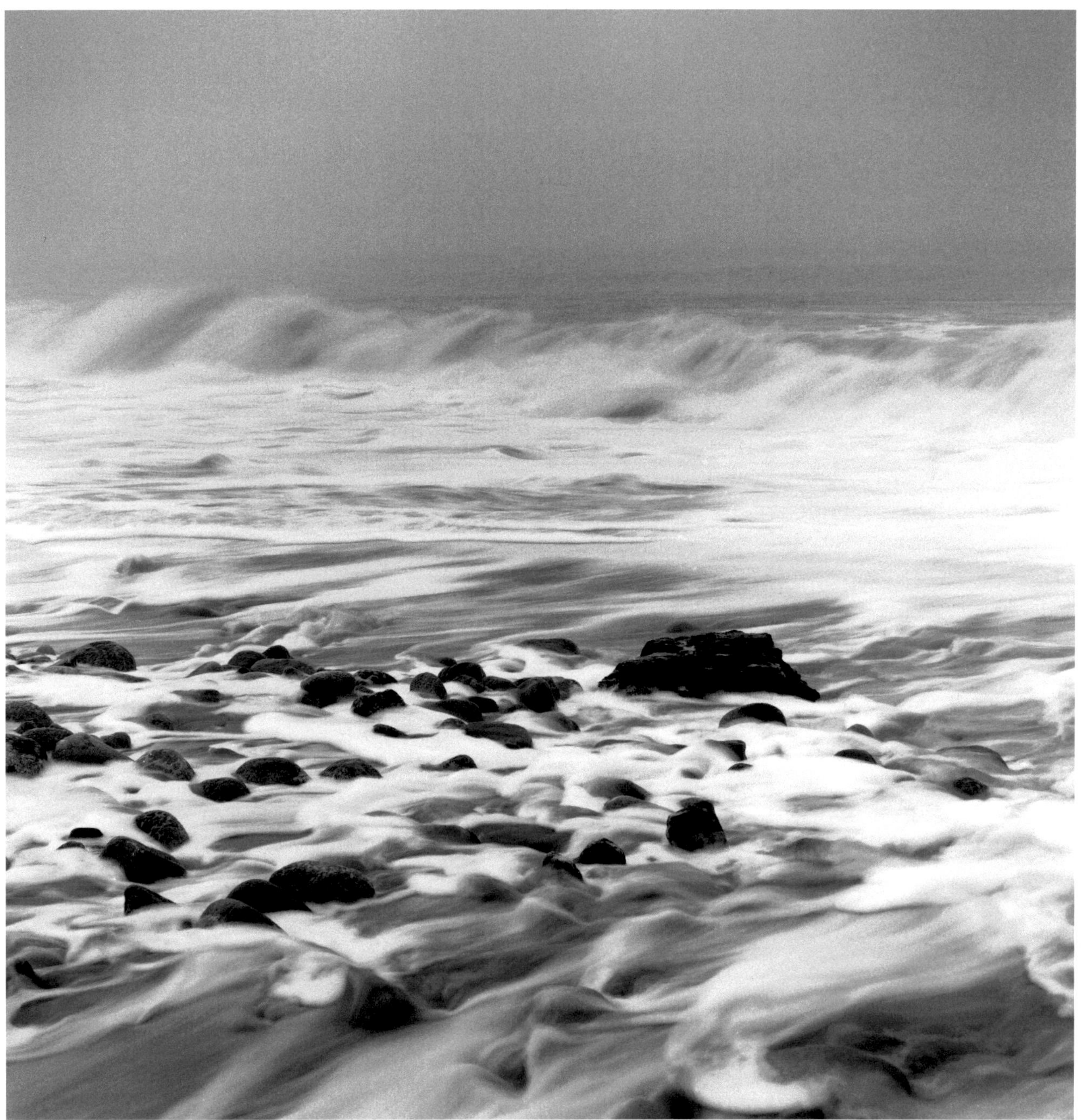

Martha's Vineyard, Massachusetts, 2017

*A river cuts through rock,
not because of its power, but
because of its persistence.*

———————————————

—JIM WATKINS

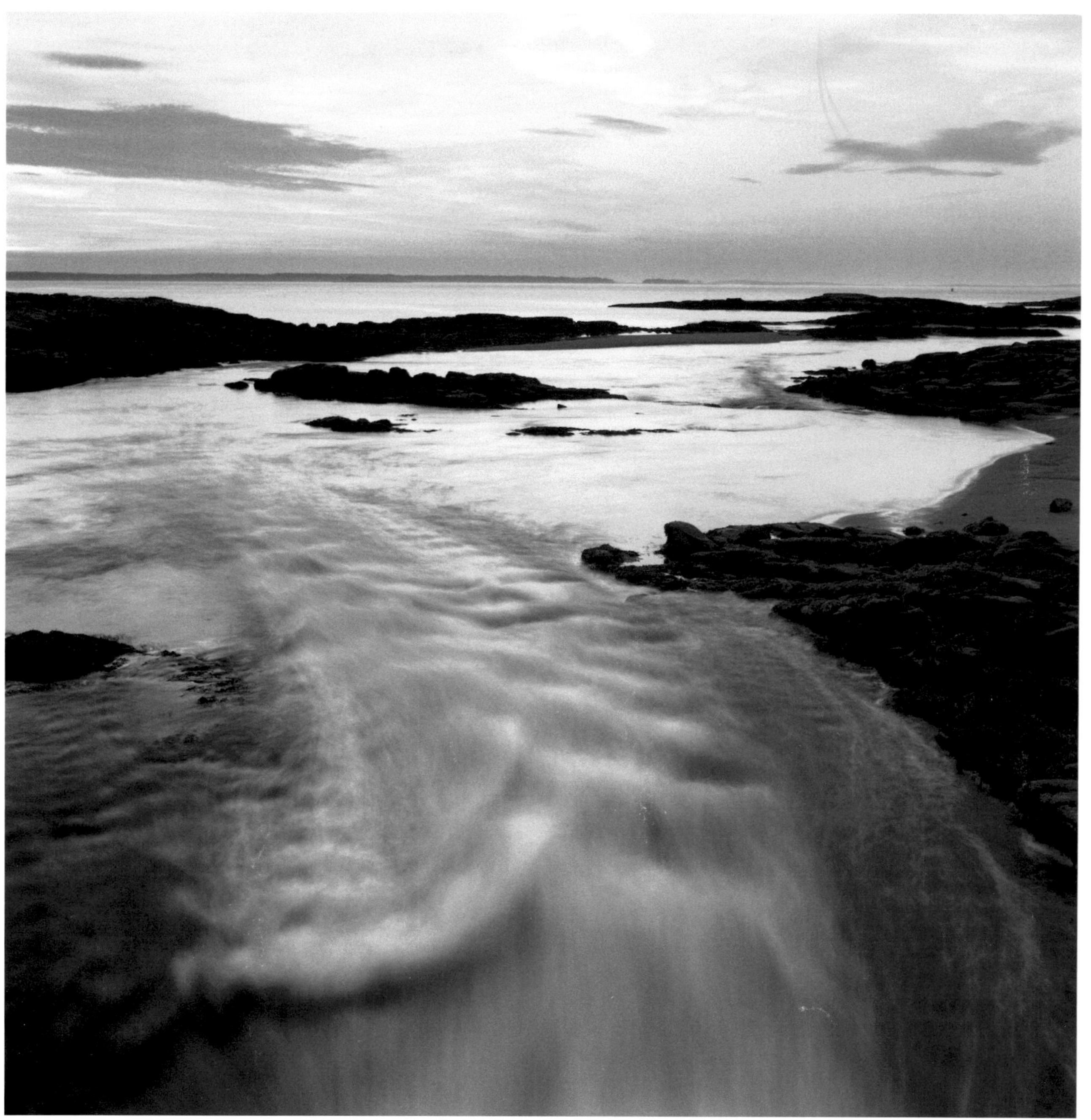

Reid State Park, Maine, 2002

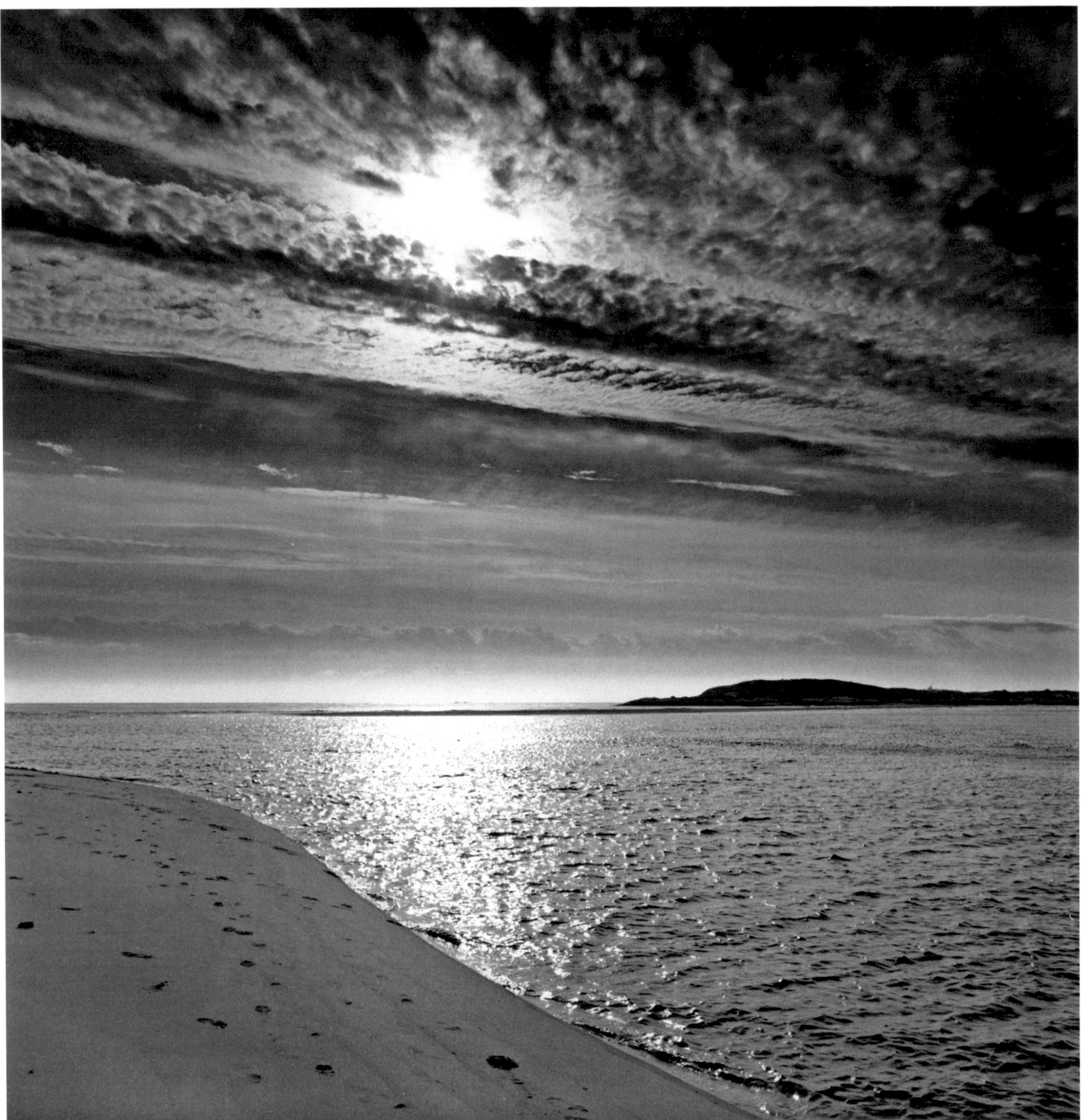

Popham Beach State Park, Maine, 2012

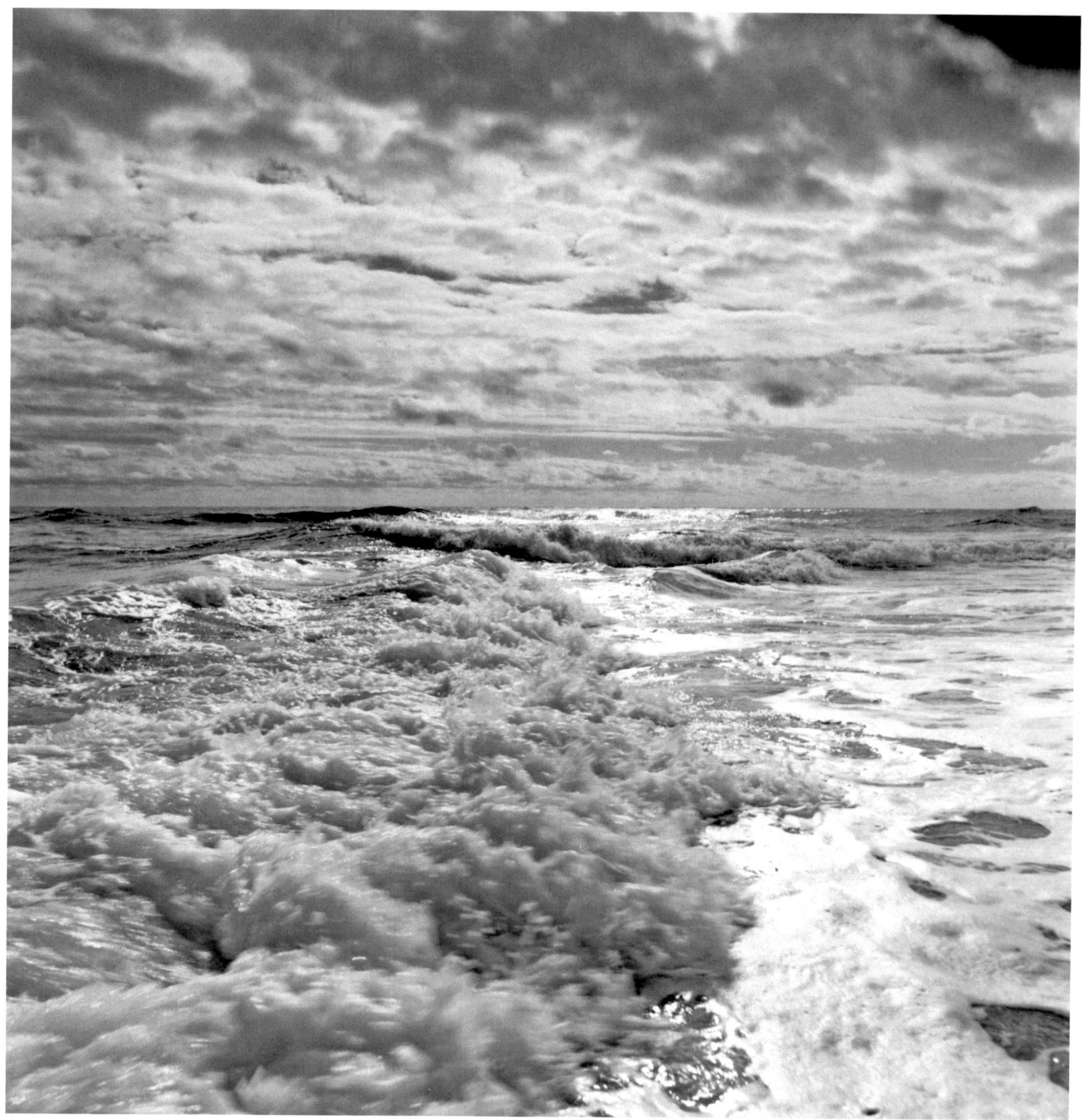

Topsail Beach, North Carolina, 2017

*I don't want life to be anything
other than what it is.*

—HERMAN HESSE

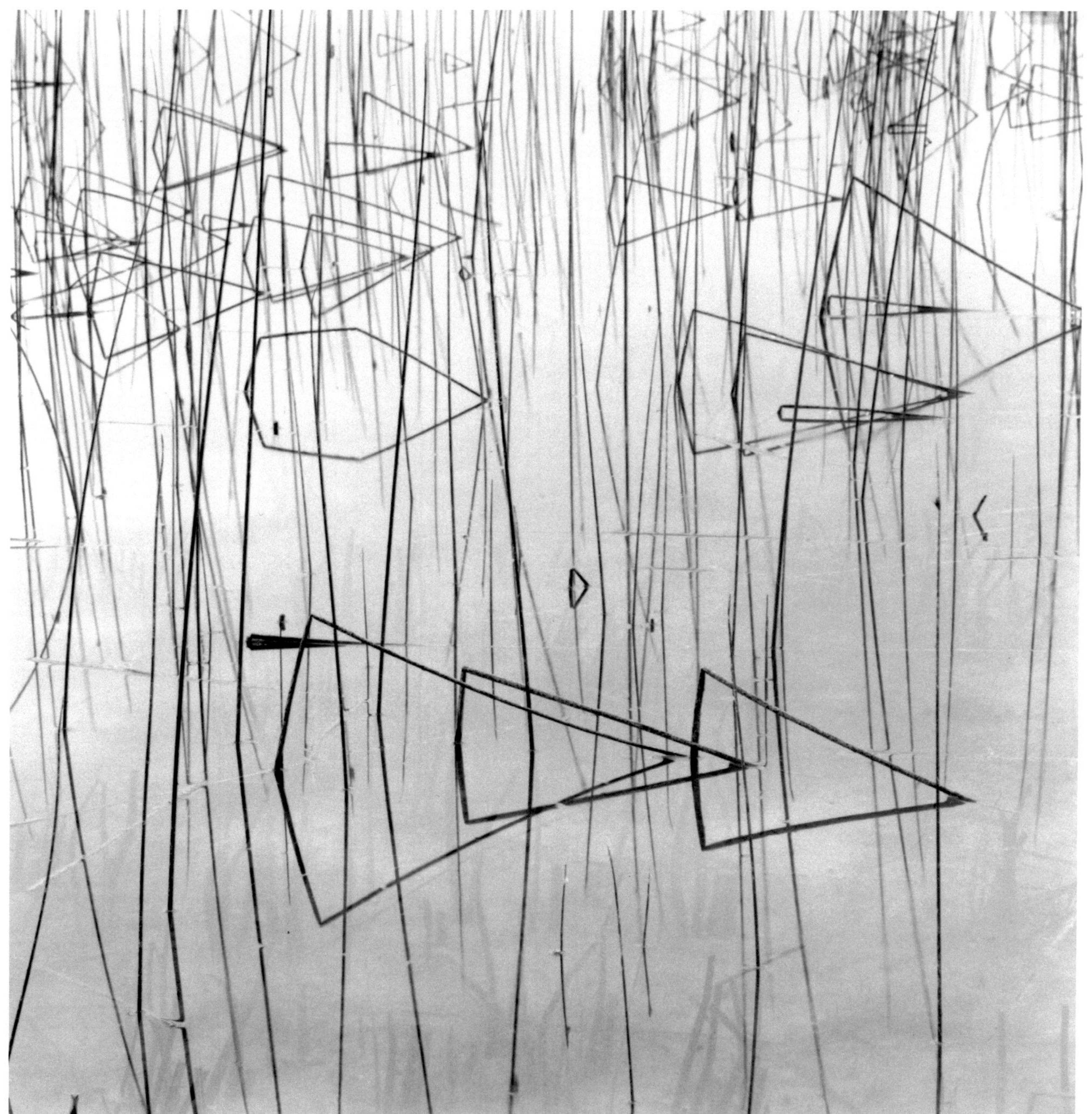

Otter Lake, Sleeping Bear Dunes National Park, Michigan, 2019

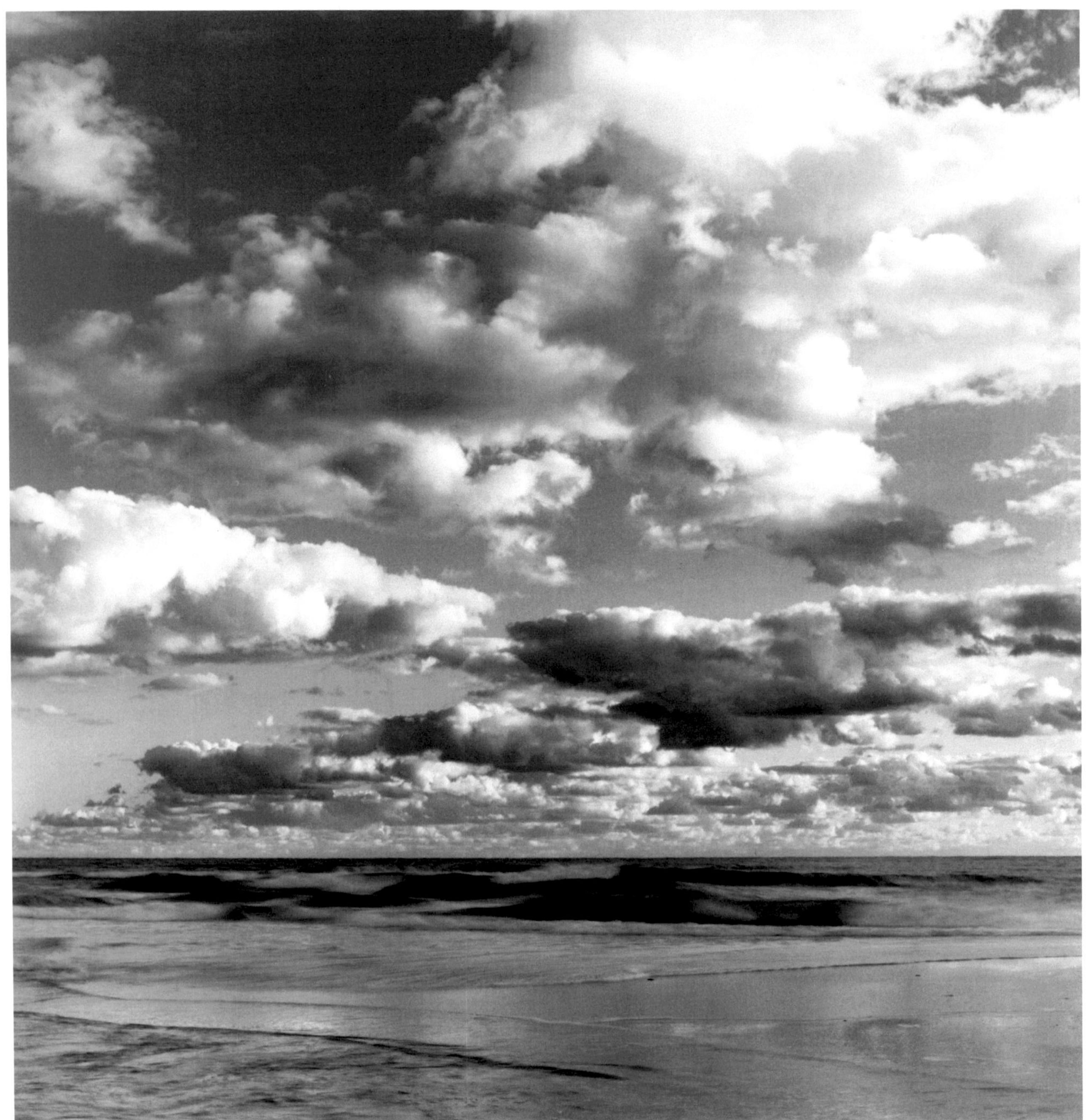

Martha's Vineyard, Massachusetts, 2001

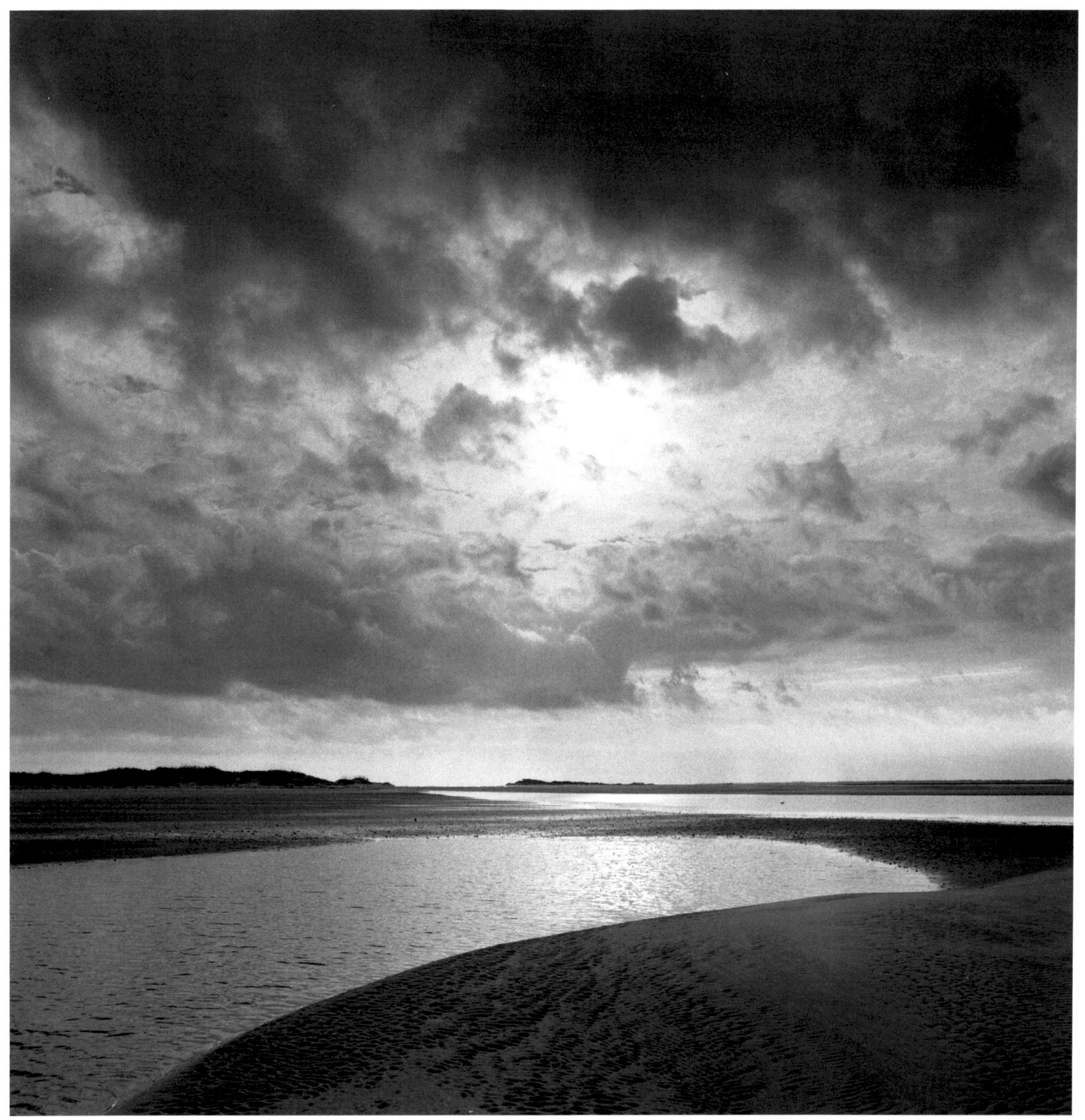

Martha's Vineyard, Massachusetts, 2007

REMEMBERING

RAINER MARIA RILKE

And you wait. You wait for the one thing
that will change your life,
make it more than it is—
something wonderful, exceptional,
stones awakening, depths opening to you.

In the dusty bookstalls
old books glimmer gold and brown.
You think of lands you journeyed through,
of paintings and a dress once worn
by a woman you never found again.

And suddenly you know: that was enough.
You rise and there appears before you
in all its longings and hesitations
the shape of what you lived.

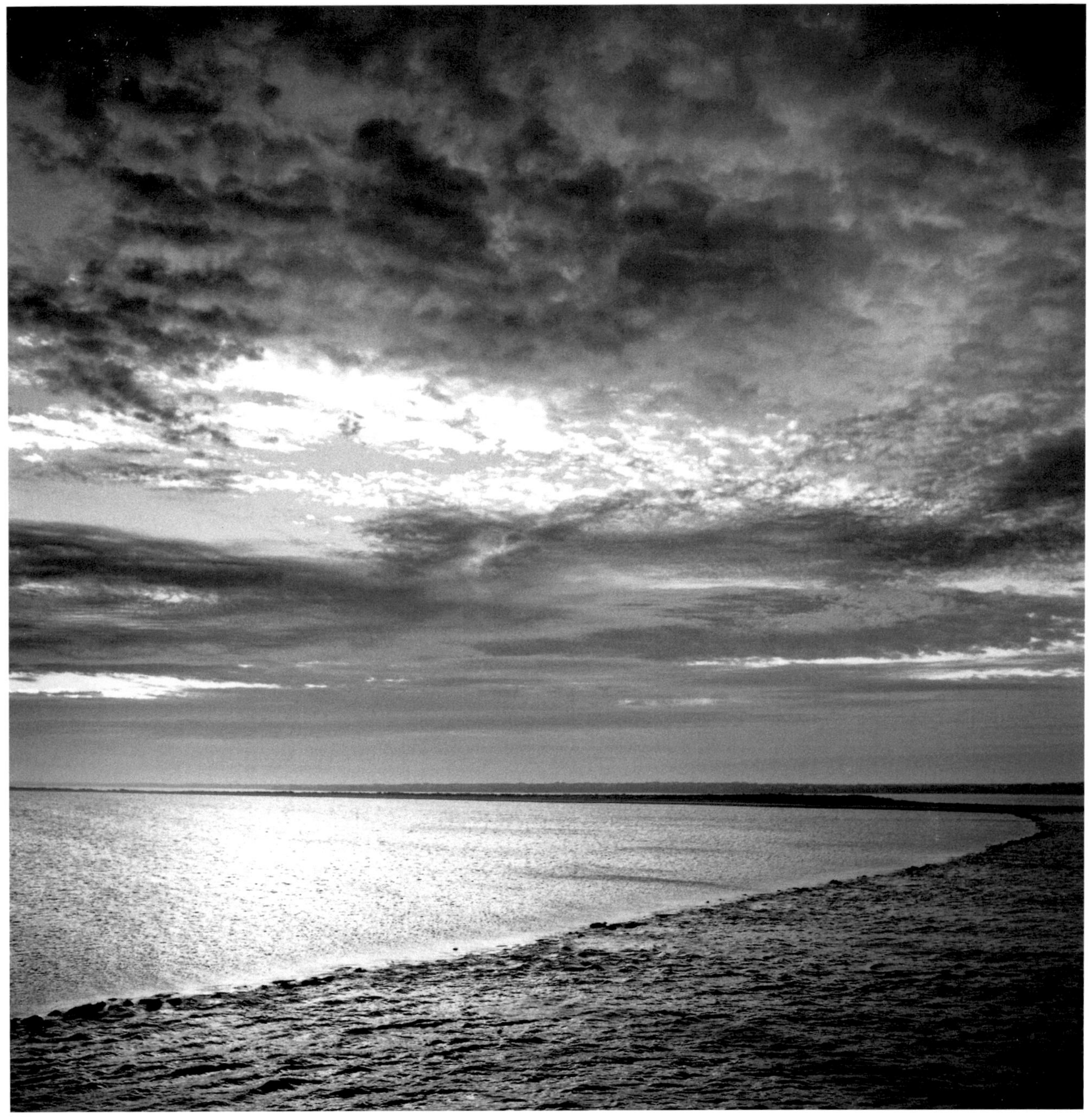

Nantucket, Massachusetts, 2005

About the Authors

Internationally renowned photographer Michael Kahn's seascape and sailing photographs are exhibited in art galleries and museums throughout the world. Captured on a 1950s camera, the images are hand-produced as silver gelatin prints and finished to museum standards.

Christine Yurick is a poet and the founding editor of *Think Journal*. Along with being Michael's wife, she is the studio manager at Michael Kahn Photography. She enjoys pairing photographs with words and sharing their combined beauty with others.

For more information, please visit www.michaelkahn.com.

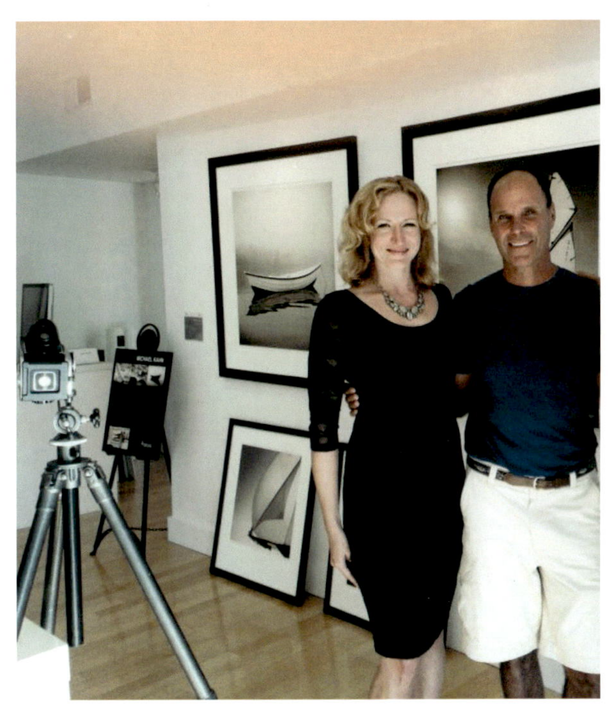